HIS PERFECT LEGACY
A Murder Mystery

By
BARBARA H. MARTIN

His Perfect Crime Trilogy
Book III

This is a work of fiction. Names, characters, businesses, places, events and incidents are either the products of the author's imagination or used in a fictitious manner. Any resemblance to actual persons, living or dead, or actual events is purely coincidental.

All drugs and their effects mentioned in this book are fictitious and are the product of the author's imagination. Any resemblance to actual drugs is purely coincidental.

Dedicated to my grandsons Joshua, Caleb and Jeremy

Special Acknowledgements
My special thanks to Delores Chancellor for her tireless effort in editing this book.

All rights reserved under International and Pan-American Copyright Conventions. By payment of required fees, you have been granted the non-exclusive, non-transferable right to access and read the text of this e-book on-screen. No part of this book may be reproduced, transmitted, downloaded, decompiled, reverse engineered, or stored in or introduced into any information storage and retrieval system, in any form or by any means, whether electronic or mechanical – except in the case of brief quotations in articles or reviews - without the express written permission of Barbara H. Martin. To contact the author, please send an email to Barbara Martin at barbara@BarbaraHMartin.com.

Copyright © 2014 by Barbara H. Martin

Cover artist credit: SelfPubBookCovers.com/Fantasyart

Other titles by Barbara H. Martin:

When the East Wind Blows

Silk Sheets and Other Things That Don't Work

The Little Book of Miracles

Walking in Power

His Perfect Crime Trilogy

His Perfect Victim

His Perfect Target

His Perfect Legacy

Contact Barbara directly at:

barbara@BarbaraHMartin.com

www.BarbaraHMartin.com

Chapter 1

It was a cold, blustery Friday in January. The pale disk of the sun had disappeared behind gray, heavy clouds, waiting to release their heavy burden of snow.

The group of people had come into the offices of Norton, Bradshaw and Holloway filled with expectation. There were twelve of them sitting around a large, oval table. Latimer took a place at the very end. He had no idea why he was here. The call had come two days ago. Gary Norton's secretary had called to invite him to the reading of the Will of William Carl Hellman, a well known wealthy stock broker and philanthropist in the city of Glenridge. Latimer didn't know any of the people in the room, but guessed they were his children and their spouses. He hadn't known William Hellman either and was surprised when the lawyer's secretary called for him to be present. He couldn't imagine what this was all about.

Gary Norton walked into the room with a black briefcase in his hand. He took out a CD and inserted it into a player.

"Before I play this, I wish to offer my condolences to the family on the death of your husband and father. He was a kind, generous man who will be greatly missed. He made this, his last Will, in my presence and two witnesses at his house four weeks ago. I attest that he was of sound mind in every sense of the word. This is one of the most unusual Wills I have ever been asked to draw up. However, I'm bound to carry it out according to Mr. Hellman's wishes. As part of the Will, I need to let you know, should any of you contest it, you will automatically be disinherited and your part will be given to charity.

Before I start, let me introduce you to Robert Latimer, owner and operator of a private detective agency in Glenridge. He is here at the request of Mr. Hellman. The reason will be explained by Mr. Hellman on the tape I will play for you in a moment." He unfolded a legal document. "Before I go on, allow me to read some sections of the Will."

He turned toward the group. "I leave my estate and all it's content, as well as fifty million dollars, to my wife, Patricia.

The sum of one hundred thousand dollars is to be distributed to each of the two homeless shelters in Glenridge. Another one hundred thousand will be given to New Life Church to be used for missionary workers in foreign countries.

The sum of fifty-thousand dollars will go to Henry Gossomer for his twenty years of faithful service as my butler. Another fifty-thousand will go to Grace Harriett, my secretary. Twenty-thousand is to be given to my friend Karl Rockwell.

"The lawyer continued on for quite a while until all the numerous large and small donations were mentioned. The group was getting restless. When he was finally done, he cleared his throat. "Before we go any further, I give all of you who I have mentioned, except his wife, the option to leave for the playing of the recording Mr. Hellman made for his children." He pushed a button after no one made a move to leave the room.

The picture of a gray-haired man in his seventies appeared on the screen. He seemed tired and ill, but alert. His piercing, blue eyes looked into the camera with sadness. There was no smile or warmth in his demeanor as he began to speak.

"By the time you hear this, I will be gone. I have lived a good life and the Lord has blessed most of my endeavors. While I'm ready to face death, I must confess, it has been devastating for me to know one of you killed me. I know it will look like I died from natural causes, but I didn't. I don't know which one of you did it. Since that is the case, I have asked Robert Latimer to find out for me which one of you couldn't wait for me to die.

I have made ample provision for Mr. Latimer to use any means necessary to discover my killer. Until then, you, my children, will not inherit anything. If the case does not get solved, your part of the inheritance will not be available to you until ten years from this day. I would therefore suggest you help him as much as you can.

Just in case you're wondering how much there is. The last time I checked, after all the other bequests have been distributed, the sum of two hundred million dollars is waiting to be divided equally among the four of you. The one who murdered me will get nothing.

I love you all and want to say something to each of you.

William, you're my oldest son. I know you have not been perfect, but neither have I. I'm proud of your achievements in your field of medicine. I wish you were a better husband and father. Work isn't everything, family is. I want you to think about spending more time with your wife and children. Forgive me for having been a bad example to you in this area. With the money you'll inherit, you should be able to cut down on your schedule and give more attention to your family.

Grant, what can I say? You are the wild one of the bunch. When you were seventeen, wild looked great, now that you're in your thirties, it wears on those around you. It's time you grow up and make something of yourself. Buying a new car every six months does not constitute responsibility. I know you have the intelligence. It's the discipline you're lacking. I had great hopes for you to finish school and go into the financial sector. I'm sorry I failed to teach you that the only way to succeed in life is through hard work. Forgive me.

Rebecca, my sweet daughter, you have pulled at my heart strings since you were born. How good it would be if you could find a man who is not after your money, but loves you for the sweet, wonderful girl you are. There isn't much wisdom in you in that area. I would have loved for you to have finished your education and become a lawyer. Instead, you've wasted your years so far on worthless endeavors to please yourself. I have failed to instill in you self confidence, because I indulged you too much. Forgive me. My advice to you is, go back to school and make something of yourself.

Sylvia, you are my strong, intelligent daughter. You will stop at nothing in order to succeed. You are a chip off the old block. There is nothing you cannot accomplish if you make up your mind. This is good, but you have forgotten about your heart. I know you've been hurt and have grown a wall around you. Allow yourself to be human and soft, and even vulnerable sometimes. What you need is to find a good man to show you what real love looks like. I'm sorry I've failed to be a good role model for you in that area. Forgive me.

Allan, my youngest, your mother has spoiled and pampered you to the point you are incapable of functioning in the real world. Your selfishness keeps you from being the wonderful person you could be. Try to do something with the riches you've been given, other than thinking of yourself. I would suggest you help those in need or volunteer to see how the other side of the world lives. I have failed to make you see, that giving is better than receiving. My heart breaks, knowing, that one of you killed me. I want you to know I forgive you. But at the same time, you will have to learn there are consequences to what we do with our life and the choices we make. When you do, I hope you will ask forgiveness from a loving God. That is worth more in eternity than all the money I could ever leave you. Do not look at this as punishment, but as the only way I know, to give you the chance to redeem your soul. Goodbye and God bless all of you."

There was silence in the room. Latimer sat, stunned. He had no idea how the man got his name or why he would have chosen him for such a task. He was waiting for the lawyer to give him some of that information.

A low murmur filled the room. He looked at the people. They were trying to cope with the idea one of them might have killed their father. Latimer could see the shock on their faces. There were some who looked angry, because they had just been told they wouldn't inherit anything for a while, even ten years, if he couldn't solve the case.

"Mr. Latimer, I need to speak with you." It was Gary Norton. "Would you be so kind to follow me to my office?"

When they got there, he pointed to a chair in front of his large desk. The desk was filled with stacks of files and papers.

"Please, have a seat. I really thank you for coming. I realize this was highly unusual, but that is the way Mr. Hellman wanted it." He shuffled some papers until he found the folder he was looking for. "Mr. Hellman has given you a large amount of money to solve this case. Half of it, if you take it on, I will give you today. The rest when you solve it. Here is the check." He handed it to Latimer.

"I think that'll be sufficient Mr. Norton," Latimer said after he checked the amount. It was indeed a very large sum. "Can you tell me how Mr. Hellman heard about me?"

"I think he spoke with the Police Commissioner. He's the one who recommended you."

"I retired from the Glenridge Major Crime Unit after thirty years with the rank of Inspector," Latimer said. "My agency has only been opened for a few months. I can't tell you I have unlimited staff or a large office. I hope that is still alright with you."

"It doesn't matter what I think, Mr. Latimer. It is you Mr. Hellman requested in his Will. The large retainer should make your decision easy." He smiled.

"Do you have any idea why Mr. Hellman thinks one of his children murdered him?" Latimer asked.

"I talked to him about that when we discussed the Will. He refused to say. All he mentioned was that he would be dead soon. After he passed away, I told the coroner and the police to check carefully for any wrongdoing. Unfortunately, I could not discuss with them what was in the Will or what Mr. Hellman had said. That was all I could do to maintain client confidentiality."

"I presume the children will be ready and willing to talk to me, given the terms of the Will."

"I imagine so. After all, there is a lot of money at stake if they don't," Gary Norton said.

"I just finished a case, so I have the time to devote to this one," Latimer said. "Do you have any information that would be useful to me? I do need a list of the names, phone numbers and addresses of the five siblings."

"My secretary will provide you with that, and anything else I can do to help you solve this case."

"I would like to talk to you about Mr. Hellman. What kind of man was he? What were his business enterprises, details about his family, and other things that will help me get a better understanding of the man. If you don't have time today, maybe I can get an appointment with you as soon as possible." Latimer got up to leave.

"I don't have time today, but I'll have my secretary give your office a call as soon as I'm free." He stood and came around the desk and shook Latimer's hand. "Thank you for coming. I hope you will solve this case soon."

On the way back to his office Latimer thought about the new case. It certainly was unusual. The large retainer was more than he had ever made in a year as Inspector. However, it wasn't just the money. This case sounded fascinating. It was always astounding how many skeletons there were in the closet with a family like this. The fact, that the inheritance would be delayed for ten years if he didn't solve the case, certainly put pressure not only on him, but on the members of the family as well. He was sure it would no doubt encourage the innocent to tell all.

Latimer drove up to his office. It was a small building, just outside of downtown Glenridge. The sign on the door read LATIMER

DETECTIVE AGENCY. He nodded to Sue Ellen Kendrick, his secretary, as he walked in.

"You've been gone quite a while, Latimer darlin'," she said in a lilting Georgia drawl. She was tall, with long black hair, a narrow face and smooth skin. Her brown eyes and a ready smile made up for her unusually loud voice. "Do we have a new case?"

"We do, Sue Ellen. It's a big one." He told her what happened.

"Lordy mercy. That sounds mighty strange. That poor man, not knowing which of his kids killed him. I tell you one thing, Latimer, they don't have strange goings on like that in Adell, Georgia. Folks don't have as much money there, but they don't carry on like these city folks neither."

"I brought a list of the people I need to interview. They are Mr. Hellman's children and their spouses, if they have any. I want you to call them and make an appointment with each one. Make sure my recorder is ready to go before I leave."

"You want to talk to every one of them Monday?"

"It doesn't have to be, but in view of the circumstances, they will be eager to talk to me. Give me at least an hour for each plus travel time."

"Will do, darlin'."

"There is one more thing, Sue Ellen. Find out who the coroner is. I need the report when it's ready. I don't know when the man died, but I imagine the findings should be available by now. Another thing, I need to visit William Hellman's house and go over it with a fine tooth comb. Call his wife and ask her when I can do that and interview her at the same time." He walked into his office and sat behind his desk.

"That'll keep me busy for a while." Sue Ellen stood in the doorway to Latimer's office. "I have a date tonight. I need to get out of here on time."

"Is it the slick guy from the garage?"

"His name is Wayne Morris. And he ain't slick at all. He's a nice guy. We're going steady." She was beaming.

Latimer smiled. Sue Ellen was certainly not your average, everyday secretary. She described every person who called the office in her own unique style before she connected them to Latimer. Her folksy phrases never failed to amuse him. In spite of her country ways, she was intelligent and wise in her assessment of situations and people. The best part about Sue Ellen was her Georgia accent. It made even the worst news easier to deal with.

He looked at his office. Maybe he could make some improvements with the money he made with this case. The room was sparsely furnished. There was a large desk and two straight chairs in front of it. A shelf in back was filled with legal books, a few files and several large, black binders. A lopsided, plastic feather palm stood in one corner, ready to fall over at any moment. It reminded him of his honeymoon in Florida last year.

His eyes turned to the picture of a middle-aged woman with beautiful, silver-gray hair and a warm smile. It was his wife Glenda. He picked up the frame and remembered the wonderful honeymoon they spent at a plush condo in West Palm Beach. It belonged to Cassandra Helen Anscott, the sole heiress to Anscott Research Laboratories, a large company with medical Labs and research facilities all down the East coast. Latimer, when he was still an Inspector with the Glenridge Major Crime Unit, had solved the murder of Cassie's father, Patrick Anscott. The case drew nationwide attention. In the process Latimer met Glenda, Patrick Anscott's personal assistant. After Cassie took on a larger responsibility at the firm, she asked Glenda to be her assistant. All of them remained close friends, especially since Latimer had saved Cassie's life during a dramatic incident at the end of the case.

Since his retirement from the Glenridge Major Crime Unit, Latimer and Glenda had made a number of new friends through another case referred to him by Cassie. Latimer solved it where the Crime Unit had failed. That must be why the Police Commissioner had recommended him to Mr. Hellman.

Glenda and Latimer lived in a nice condo outside of Glenridge. It had been hers when they got married. The only thing he brought from his place was his favorite chair. Latimer's wife Mary had died eleven years ago of cancer and Glenda was the first woman he dated after that. Glenda's husband had left her for a younger woman and it had hurt her deeply. She never wanted to trust another man, until she met Latimer. It had been a fabulous wedding, given by Cassie at the Anscott Estate. Since then, Cassie had married Jeremy Sanders a month ago. They just returned from their honeymoon in Aruba. The two seemed a mismatched pair. She was a wealthy heiress and he a lowly IT manager at Bellami Trucking, Inc. They had met during the last case Latimer had solved.

The phone interrupted his musings.

"It's that lovely wife of yours, Latimer," Sue Ellen shouted from her desk just outside the door.

"Hi, honey," Glenda said. "I just want to let you know we're invited to the Estate for dinner. We are celebrating Cassie's and Jerry's return. Make sure you're home in time. Dinner is at eight."

Chapter 2

Latimer drove up to their condo in the suburb of Hollow Grove. The doorman greeted him with a smile as he walked by and took the elevator to the second floor.

"Hi Sweetheart, I'm glad you're home." After ten years of coming home to an empty house, he loved being greeted by Glenda. She was in her early sixties, not thin, but trim and healthy looking. Dark blue eyes spoke of a keen intelligence. Her silver-gray hair was cut in a short, stylish way. Skillfully applied make-up hid her years well, except for tiny wrinkles around her eyes, especially when she smiled.

"Hello, handsome." She brushed his cheek with a kiss. Latimer was taller than she and had a full head of gray hair with a well-trimmed beard and gray eyes to match. He was a man of substance. While not overweight, a little exercise wouldn't hurt, Glenda emphasized frequently. He presented a picture of authority, softened by a deep, soft voice and a wonderful sense of humor. The sudden twinkle in his eyes made it easy for him to relate to the people he dealt with in his job.

"Is this all I get?" He grabbed her and hugged her. "You are still the prettiest woman I know."

"I'm glad you think so. I'm trying very hard to make sure I do look pretty for tonight. Peter and Andrea Bellami will be there as well. I suppose we will find out how the honeymoon went for Cassie and Jerry. I hope they are happy."

"What's not to like about a honeymoon?" Latimer said with a twinkle in his eyes. "It hasn't been that long ago since we celebrated ours." He pulled her close and kissed her.

"We have to get ready, honey," she said as she pushed him away with a smile. "You're still a lecherous old man, Bob. I can't say I mind."

The gate to the Estate rolled away silently. Latimer was still impressed with the tree-lined driveway up to the big house. It was a three-story mansion with six columns reaching to the second floor. A row of white, framed windows across the front accentuated the gray exterior. In the summer, large planters with lush, green plants stood between the columns, which gave the mansion a touch of elegance. They had been removed indoors for the winter. Four garages were attached to the house on one side. The front was lit up by ornate, antique lamps across the front. It was eight o'clock and the beautiful, large grounds lay hidden in the dark.

The massive front door was opened by Richard McAllister. With his 6'4' frame and full head of white hair, the man presented the perfect picture of a butler. His dark suit hung on him flawlessly.

"Inspector and Mrs. Latimer, it is wonderful to see you. Please, come in. Cassie and Jerry are in the morning room with Mr. and Mrs. Bellami," he said in his formal British accent.

"Hello Richard. How is Emily? We are looking forward to seeing her again and can't wait for her delicious cooking," Glenda said.

"She will be delighted to see you as well."

Emily was Richard's wife. The two of them ran the house and had been in the employment of the Anscott family for twenty years. When Cassie lost her family last year, she had rewarded the couple with a large trust fund. It was enough so they would never have to work again. They stayed on because of their love for Cassie and she made them a part of the family.

"Here they are. It's about time you guys got here. We want to hear about your new case, Bob." It was Cassie. She was twenty-seven, with long, wavy auburn hair, cut in a mid-length style. Her piercing blue eyes were a gift from her father. She wore flawless make-up and her slender figure looked fit in designer jeans with a matching sweater. She was beaming.

"I guess I don't have to ask how the honeymoon went. Just by looking at you I can tell it must have been great," Latimer said as he hugged her. "You look absolutely radiant, girl."

"We are happy, aren't we, Jerry?" She turned to her new husband.

"I still can't believe she loves me," Jerry said with his typical boyish grin. He was tall and lanky, with a wild shock of blond hair and wonderfully warm, blue eyes. He was dressed in jeans and a t-shirt. "I'm a happy camper. She made me buy a bunch of clothes I'll never wear, but at least I can say I have them." His remark brought a round of laughter. Jerry was a lovable, friendly, easy-going computer guy, who owned nothing but jeans and t-shirts when he met Cassie. Everybody knew he was the most sloppy, worst dressed man in the world. He would have been late to the dinner tonight, if it wasn't at his house. The social differences between him and his new wife were enormous. Jerry came from a solid, lower middle class background. His parents were of modest means. To live in his wife's wealthy surroundings would be quite an adjustment for him. He had thought long and hard if he could handle Cassie being the one with the money in their relationship. There could be no doubt, however, he did not marry Cassie for her money. It simply didn't mean that much to him. He loved his family and was proud of his wonderful parents and his siblings.

Jerry was IT manager at Bellami Trucking, Inc. and had every intention to work for a living, just like he had done before. Peter Allan Bellami was his boss. Jerry and Peter had known each other for many years and were college buddies and best friends. Cassie and Peter's wife, Andrea, had been close for several years as well.

Latimer and Glenda were the newcomers in this group. The younger set accepted them, as well as Richard and Emily, as their surrogate family members and included them in all their social gatherings.

"How was your trip?" Latimer asked.

"We had a wonderful time. Jerry never once had to dress up. We enjoyed the ocean and some of the many restaurants. We met some nice people and were invited to parties and beach picnics. It was fun." Cassie looked happy as she took Jerry's hand.

"It was great, but I'm glad to be back." He looked around the beautiful morning room. "I suppose this will be it from now on. It'll take some getting used to."

"It doesn't look to me like you'll be suffering, old boy," Peter said with a grin. Everybody laughed.

"Dinner is served," Richard announced.

"Now tell us about your new case," Cassie said when they were seated at the table. "I heard about it from Glenda."

"The whole thing was very strange. I was asked to come to the reading of the Will of William Carl Hellman. In a video he told his family that someone killed him. He suspected it was one of his children. He asked me to solve the murder. If I don't, his kids won't get their millions for ten years." Latimer leaned back in his chair. "That puts a lot of pressure on me to get results."

"I know Bill Hellman and his wife Patricia," Cassie said. "They are nice people. My father was good friends with them. My mom was close to Patricia for many years, but then they grew apart. The Hellman's travelled a lot and Pat didn't have time to socialize a whole lot locally."

"I've never heard of a crazy Will like that," Andrea said. "How does he know one of his kids did it? And why didn't he say who he thought it was and why?"

"According to his lawyer, he didn't know. He said in his video that the police and coroner wouldn't find anything wrong, but he was convinced he would be murdered. I'm going to the coroner's office for the results of the autopsy on Monday," Latimer said. "It sounds like a very interesting and challenging case. Cassie, I may want to ask you a few more questions about the family. Maybe you have some idea which of the children would be capable of murder."

"I know some of them. We ran around in the same circles when we grew up. I'll start getting my thoughts together and call you if I have something interesting in that area," Cassie said. She turned to Richard. "Is Emily coming to sit with us?"

"She'll be here momentarily, Cassie," he said.

At that moment Emily walked in. She was a short, rotund woman with curly, gray hair and a reddish face. It turned into countless little wrinkles when she smiled. Her blue eyes had a warm sparkle to them. In her early sixties, she was still energetic and full of life.

"Here ye are, my favorite Inspector and his lovely wife," she said with a delightful Irish accent. "I miss not having ye here with us anymore."

Glenda and Latimer had stayed at the Estate during the last murder case, since there had been a threat on their lives by the murderer. After that, Cassie insisted they remain until she got married.

"Your cooking is as good as ever, Emily," Glenda said. "I'm having a hard time competing with you, now that we live in our condo again."

"I'm going to get fat," Jerry said. "This is like having my mom's cooking every day." He looked around with a grin.

"What are you going to call yourself, now that you're married, Cassie?" Latimer asked.

"We have decided I'm going to be Mrs. Cassandra Helen Anscott Sanders." She beamed. "I really like the sound of that."

"It's a mouth full." Jerry laughed. "But in her circles, I think it'll do."

"Just remember, they are our circles now," Cassie said. "As a matter of fact, there will be a formal function at the company in honor of our wedding. It'll be held at the Granger Hotel in two weeks, and you, my dear husband, will have to really dress up for the occasion. It'll be a chance for everyone to get to know you."

"Holy mackerel, that sounds horrible. I better take some lessons on how to behave between now and then." He turned to Richard. "You know how, Richard. Will you teach me some of the finer points of society?"

"I certainly will, Jerry. Whenever you wish to start, I'll be ready," Richard said. "I think that sounds like a wonderful idea."

"Why don't we get started tomorrow? I definitely don't want to embarrass Cassie." He looked at the rest of the group. "It'll be one of those dinners with fifteen forks and seven knives and spoons and I'll be the only one who doesn't know which one to use." He sighed deeply.

Cassie laughed. "It won't be that bad, but I think it does sound like a good idea, Richard."

"Just don't complain, like you normally do, that you couldn't come in jeans and t-shirt," Andrea said. "That wouldn't go over very well in that crowd."

It turned out to be a great evening. It was quite late when Latimer and Glenda were driving home.

"I'm a little concerned how Jerry is going to do with this new lifestyle," Glenda said. "The man hates these high society functions. The difference between their two worlds is enormous."

"He better get used to them," Latimer said. "I think he'll be fine. He will adjust because he loves Cassie. When he gets enough of it, they can always go and visit his family. That'll bring everything back into focus." Latimer sounded confident.

It was Monday morning. Latimer shivered in the icy rain as he got out of the car in front of his office. A cup of coffee would feel good. Sue Ellen was already there.

"Good mornin', Latimer. It's mighty nasty out there."

He nodded and went into his office.

"Did you get those appointments I asked for on Friday, Sue Ellen?"

"I got two of them and will work on the others today, boss." She walked in and put two slips of paper on his desk. "One is from the doctor. He's got a craw in his throat, real short and businesslike." She stood in front of his desk and handed him a cup of coffee. "Here, you need it this mornin'. You sound just like him." She smiled. "The other one is the wife, a real sweet thing and very friendly."

"Which one is it, the old or the young Mrs. Hellman?"

"It's the old one at the big house."

"Thanks, Sue Ellen. I'm sorry. I think the weather is getting to me. It's hard to come back from Florida into this cold and dreary mess. Then again, now that I look at you, you're like a ray of Georgia sunshine. You must've had a date with your garage man this weekend." He smiled at her.

"I sure did. We had more fun than a coon dog chasing a rabbit."

He loved Sue Ellen's folksy expressions. They didn't always make sense to him, but they cheered him up.

"Did Mr. Norton's office call Friday?"

"No, they didn't."

"Why don't you give them a call? I need to speak with him and get some more information about the Hellman family members."

Latimer leaned back in his chair, coffee in hand. This was an unusual case. He had to establish several things before he could solve it. First, find out if a murder had been committed. What if William Hellman was wrong and he really did die of natural causes, like the coroner's report seemed to indicate. Second, if it was a homicide, it didn't necessarily mean one of the children had committed it. Third, the old man could've had a senile moment and imagined the whole thing. If indeed it was murder, with this much money involved, the motive would most certainly be greed.

To make sure about these facts, he had to talk to the family. They held the key. Before he took on a case, Latimer liked to find out what kind of a person the victim was. He wanted to know his background, business, character, friends, enemies as well as weaknesses and strengths. It helped him get a feel for the case. His first appointment was this morning with Mrs. Patricia Hellman.

"Sue Ellen, do you have the address for Mrs. Hellman?"

"I do, Latimer. It's a little ways out of town in an exclusive, secluded area. I wish I could go with you and see it." Sue Ellen sounded awed. "I put the address on the paper I gave you, darlin'." She called everyone she liked darlin'.

It took thirty minutes to get there. A large, wrought-iron gate guarded the entrance. He got out and pushed the button.

"Robert Latimer here to see Mrs. Hellman," he said when the intercom came on.

The gate swung back and he drove down a winding road for some time. When the large house finally came into view, it took his breath away. It was a huge, red brick, three-story mansion. A circular driveway ran along the entire front. A manicured lawn with neatly trimmed hedges surrounded a small pond. Large oak trees graced the entire area to give it a stunning effect of grace and beauty. Latimer could imagine how spectacular it would look in the summer. The home sat in the midst of rolling hills, with horse stables surrounded by white fences in the distance. Because it was winter, he did not see any horses.

The front door opened as soon as he got out of the car.

"Please come in, Mr. Latimer. Mrs. Hellman will see you now," the butler said. "Allow me to show you the way." He was a middle-aged man with dark, thin hair, a straight, pronounced nose and brown eyes. He was of medium height, slightly overweight, but immaculately dressed in a dark suit.

Latimer recognized Henry Gossomer from the meeting.

"Thank you, Henry."

The large foyer was overwhelmed by a magnificent staircase in the middle, branching out to both sides. A large chandelier hung from the high ceiling. A heavy, plush oriental carpet covered the floors and the stairs. To the left a door opened into a medium-sized room with two large windows overlooking the front lawn. It was furnished with exquisite antique furniture. Latimer wondered if the paintings by several of the masters were real. They gave the room a formal, yet warm, comfortable feeling.

"Mr. Latimer is here to see you, Madam."

A woman in her late sixties got up from a beautiful seating area and came toward Latimer.

"How nice to see you again, Mr. Latimer. I remember you from Mr. Norton's office the other day. I'm Patricia Hellman." She shook his hand and pointed to a chair. "Can Henry bring you something to drink?"

"A cup of coffee would be wonderful, Mrs. Hellman."

Without a word Henry disappeared.

"I'm still in shock about the Will my husband made. To think one of my children would murder their father is unthinkable." She looked pale. Her blond, short hair was styled in a way that brought out her high cheekbones, a thin, straight nose and bright, blue eyes. It was a face with stunning, classic features. She was slender and looked like she exercised regularly. Her tailored black pants and matching top made her look even thinner. "I don't agree with William about him being murdered. It's ridiculous, but there is nothing any of us can do but go along with this investigation, Mr. Latimer. Mind you, none of us blame you, but it is nevertheless most uncomfortable for this family to be subjected to this kind of treatment."

Henry walked in with the coffee. He poured a cup for Latimer and handed it to him.

"That will be all for now, Henry. Thank you," she said.

"Does that mean the family is pretty upset with your husband?" Latimer treaded lightly.

"It does. The children are furious and were thinking of refusing to be questioned. I guess the way the Will is written, they would get nothing if they do. So what choice do they have?" She was visibly upset.

"I can certainly understand that, Ma'am and I will try to be as discreet as possible. However, I have been hired by your husband to investigate his death and that is what I'm going to have to do." He spoke softly.

"I understand." She fumbled with her napkin. "I just hope this whole mess will be resolved soon."

"How long were you married, Mrs. Hellman?"

"Thirty-five years. Our anniversary would have been three weeks after he died."

"Can I ask you if it had been a good marriage?"

"It was like most. We had our differences, but our children kept us together."

"Does that mean you would have left him if it wasn't for them?" Latimer wondered if he had gone too far.

"No, I don't think so. William was a good man. He treated me with love and respect, and we never got to the point of divorce at any time. His religion drove me crazy at times, but at least he didn't expect me to go along with it. We had come to an understanding several years ago. He believed the way he did, and would leave me alone about it."

"How did he get along with his children?"

"There was a lot of tension at times. They spent money on things he didn't approve of and some led a lifestyle he didn't agree with. Especially my youngest son, who I felt, had a very bad attitude towards his father. It was the one big area William and I totally disagreed." She looked a little embarrassed. "I guess I spoil him terribly. He was born late in my life, and I guess I gave him too much freedom."

"Do the children have their own money?" Latimer asked.

"They do have some income, but William didn't believe in giving them too much. He wanted them to go to school and make their own way in life. He was strict that way."

"Did you agree with that?"

"No I didn't. I supplemented their income as much as I could get away with. It was the area we fought most about." She looked thoughtful. "If one of my children really did kill him, I guess it would be my fault for indulging them too much."

"What about now, are you going to continue to give them additional funds to live on until the case is solved?" Latimer asked, hoping she would answer him.

"I probably will. After all, William left me enough to live three lifetimes. Why wouldn't I share with them?"

"I thank you so much for being so upfront and honest with me, Mrs. Hellman. I'm sure this is not the last time I will have to bother you." He got up. "Thank you for your hospitality. By the way, Cassie Anscott sends her regards. She just got married and is doing well."

"My goodness, the last time I saw her she was a teenage girl. William and I were out of town for the funerals of her parents and brother. Please, tell her I wish her good luck in her marriage. After the tragedy in her family, she deserves it." She shook Latimer's hand. "Come back any time, Mr. Latimer. Henry will see you out."

Latimer decided he would come back another time to check out the house.

Chapter 3

Instead of going back to his office, Latimer went straight to the coroner's office. He found out Dr. Patricia Christianson had handled the autopsy. Pat was a good friend and he would have no trouble getting all the answers and the report from her.

"Latimer, the love of my life, it's been a long time." Dr. Christianson said with a smile. She was a woman in her fifties, dressed as usual, in jeans and boots. Her gray hair was held together at the back of her neck. Her voice was deep, almost like a man's. It matched her gruff demeanor. "What brings you here?"

"I'm looking for the results of the Hellman autopsy, Pat. If you still love me, you'll let me take a look at it." He had a twinkle in his eyes.

"I'm telling you, the only things that keep me from throwing myself at you are my bodies." She stood in front of the autopsy table with a scalpel in her hand, ready to open up a corpse. "What do you want to know about him? There was nothing unusual, he was seventy-five and died of heart failure."

"Pat, I've been asked to look into his death. According to his own words, in a video tape of his Will, he insists one of his children killed him."

"Did he say how?" She sounded incredulous.

"No, he didn't know. He did say there wouldn't be any evidence for the police or the coroner." Latimer grinned at Pat. "If you are still mad about me, you will check on that or at least tell me what could make someone have heart failure and not leave a trace of evidence."

"There are some exotic poisons. Nothing is untraceable if you know what you're looking for. Without it, it would take forever to find it. Our lab is definitely not equipped to handle it. We would have to send blood samples to a lab in California."

"How about Anscott Research Laboratories, do they do it? If you could get me a blood sample, I have someone there who could get it tested."

"I have no idea. I have never come across anything like that in Glenridge. I believe we still have some samples in the freezer. I can let you have one of them. As to the report, there is absolutely nothing in there that would help you." She looked at Latimer through her big protective face shield. "I'm sorry, but I have to spend some more time with one of my lovelies here."

Latimer left before she could slice into the dead body in front of her. He was on his way to the office before he remembered to get the blood sample. It would have to wait. Maybe he should call Cassie first and see if her company had the capability to test for exotic poisons. He dialed Glenda's number.

"Sweetheart, it's your favorite sleuth calling. Could I speak with Cassie for a minute, please?"

"Hi, honey. I will ring you through."

"Bob, what can I do for you?" Cassie sounded cheerful.

He explained the situation.

"I have no idea whether we do that, but I can find out and call you back later. Did you talk to Patricia?"

"I did and she sends her good wishes for your marriage."

"Thanks, it's been a long time since I've seen her. I'll talk to you later."

"You have an appointment later this afternoon with Rebecca Hellman," Sue Ellen said when he got back to the office. "She lives in a condo near where you and Glenda live. She will be home at four this afternoon. I told her you'll be there."

"Thanks, Sue Ellen. When was my appointment with Dr. Hellman?"

"He said he will see you tomorrow at noon at his office. It's in that big medical building right across from Glenridge Memorial."

"Did you get in touch with the other three?"

"Grant Hellman is out of town. He will be back next week. Sylvia Hellman can see you Wednesday morning at her condo and Allan, her brother, will be available at the Hellman Estate that afternoon at two. I still have not heard from the lawyer's office."

"Why don't you give them a call? I would like to talk to him first. Make it tomorrow morning if at all possible. I'm going to lunch. I'll see you later." He dialed Brighton's number at the precinct. Det. Sgt. Kevin Brighton used to be his sidekick when he was an Inspector. They worked together during his last case, after he retired from the force.

"Do you have time to go to lunch? I'll pick you up. I want to tell you about my new case," he said when Brighton answered the phone.

"That sounds great. I'll meet you in the parking lot." He sounded cheerful as ever. With his blond hair, bright blue eyes and deep dimples when he smiled, he was the perfect picture of the friendly policeman. After he worked with Latimer for three years, he was promoted to Det. Sergeant. He looked much younger than his twenty-nine years. Yet in spite of his innocent, young looks, he was a competent detective.

"I'm so glad you called," he said as he jumped into Latimer's waiting car. "This is foul weather today and I was sitting in my office doing paperwork." He gave Latimer one of his bright smiles. "Tell me about your new case. Is there anything I can do to help?"

"No, not this time," Latimer said and told him about the case.

"Good grief, that's a strange one. Did you talk to the coroner yet?"

"I talked with Pat Christianson. She will let me have a blood sample to take to Anscott Research Laboratories and see if they can check for some exotic poison that doesn't leave a trace. I called Cassie and she said she would look into it." Latimer leaned over and boxed Brighton's shoulder. "It's good to see you, son. How is it going with you?"

"I also have a new case. It's not as weird as yours, but I may call you if I get stuck."

"That's ok with me. How's Harold Brown? He's not giving you any problems is he?" Latimer asked. Brown had been in competition with Latimer who would solve the most cases before retirement. He got extremely upset when Latimer cracked a case Brown had given up.

"He stays out of my way mostly. We don't really talk. At least he doesn't try to interfere with what I'm doing. I think the Chief had a talk with him," Brighton said. "I heard he's going to retire at the end of this year."

"Are you still going to get married to Hattie Mansfield?"

"You bet. We met the family and everybody seems to like each other. Hattie wants a June wedding. That leaves a lot of time for the women to work on the preparations. It's going to be quite something from what I hear."

They had lunch at the little diner close to the precinct, their favorite place. When they said goodbye, they had no idea they would be working together again very soon.

When Latimer returned to the office, Cassie called him.

"I've made inquiries about your blood tests. I was told they do that at the New York facilities. Have the coroner send it there and I will see to it they do it. They are not a regular lab who does this for the public, but on my word, they will make an exception."

"You are wonderful, Cassie. Make sure they charge whatever they want. The Hellman estate will pay for it," Latimer said.

"I have no idea how that works, Bob. I'm sure, since I want it done, they will do it for nothing."

"How are Jerry and you adjusting to home life?" Latimer asked.

"He's at work at Bellami Trucking during the day. I think that makes things more normal for him. He also has Peter to talk to. We are happy. I'm a little worried about that big company party coming up. Do you and Glenda want to come? It might make it easier for him."

"Why don't you ask Glenda? She's in charge of our social calendar."

"I'll do that. Take care, Bob. I've got to go. Bye."

He wasn't sure he wanted to go. It would probably be a dressy affair. He only owned one real good, black suit and it had gotten a little tight lately, with Emily's good cooking and the stay at the condo in Florida over the last few weeks.

He spent the rest of the afternoon making notes of the interview with Patricia Hellman. Sue Ellen could type them up. He would take a tape recorder for the one this afternoon with Rebecca Hellman.

Before he left for the interview, he called Pat Christianson at the coroner's office and asked her if she could send the blood sample to the Anscott Research Laboratory in New York. He told her to charge him for the shipping cost. He also gave her Glenda's phone number to get a letter from Cassie to accompany the shipment. Pat told him, it would take a few days and the tests would take even longer.

"Thanks for doing this for me, Pat. I owe you one." He said.

"You owe me so many favors by now, Latimer, I pretty well own you. There is simply nothing I won't do for a handsome man." She chuckled.

Latimer left a little after three o'clock. The weather had gotten worse. Gale force winds had come up and the rain came down in sheets. He told Sue Ellen to go home before it got worse.

He arrived at Rebecca Hellman's condo with fifteen minutes to spare. The doorman told him he could leave his car under the overhang by the front door if he didn't stay longer than an hour.

"Leave the keys in the car so I can move it if someone needs the space." He smiled when Latimer gave him a big tip.

Latimer took the elevator up to the third floor. This condo building was a lot more upscale than his and Glenda's down the road. There was only one condo on the top floor when the elevator door opened. He knocked on the door.

A maid in uniform answered the door and let Latimer in.

"I will tell Ms. Hellman you are here," she said with a friendly smile.

"Mr. Latimer. I'm Rebecca Hellman. Please, call me Becky." She shook his hand. "I've been expecting you. Mother called to tell me she talked with you." She gave him a half-smile and pointed to a seating area in the large living room in front of a row of windows. Rain pelted against the panes and obstructed the breathtaking view of the rolling hills. "Please, have a seat. I'll have Rachel bring us some coffee. In this weather I'm sure you could use it."

"Thank you, Becky, I appreciate it." Latimer sat down and looked around the room. It was furnished in French provincial antiques with thick, white carpet to match. It presented a light, airy atmosphere mixed with elegance. "You have a beautiful place."

"Thank you. I love it."

She was in her late thirties. Her blond hair hung in unruly curls down to her shoulders. It surrounded an oval face with blue eyes, a tiny nose and mouth. Her skin reminded Latimer of a porcelain doll with its flawless, white complexion. He couldn't see that she used any make-up, except around the eyes and a touch of bright, pink lipstick.

"Do you mind if I tape this interview? It makes it easier for me to remember." He asked.

"That's fine with me."

Latimer took a minute to set up the recorder.

"Let me first give you my condolences on your father's death," He said.

"He was sick for quite a while and so it didn't come that much of a shock to us. What was the shock, was his Will." She looked at Latimer with a look of annoyance. "Imagine, thinking any one of us would kill our own father."

"That, of course, is the reason I'm here to talk to you. Can you tell me what kind of a man he was, Becky?"

"I loved him very much. Everybody knew I was his favorite. He doted on me from the time I was little." She giggled. "I could get anything out of him, even if Mother said 'no'. He was a big man with a big heart."

"How did the others feel about your favorite status with him?" Latimer asked.

"They all knew about it. When they wanted something he wouldn't give them, they would send me to ask him. Many times it worked." She giggled again. She reminded Latimer of a little girl, in spite of her age.

"Do you have any idea which if one of your siblings might be capable of killing him? I'm not saying any of them did, just capable."

"We're all so very different. Take William, my oldest brother. He is such a stuffy person. All he knows is his medicine. He never played much, except doctor. Father gave him a medical play set when he was five and he would run around trying to listen to our heart. He married another doctor. I bet that's all those two do is talk about medicine instead of love." She laughed. "I on the other hand think about love all the time. Father did not approve of most of the men I brought home, even when I was a teenager. He said all they wanted was my money."

"Did they?" Latimer smiled at her.

"Probably, but I didn't care as long as they treated me nice."

"Did that meet with your father's disapproval?"

"Oh yes. He would get angry with me or better, frustrated. I may look like a ditsy blond, Mr. Latimer, but I do what I want when I want." He could tell by her firm tone she meant it.

"You haven't answered my question. Who do you think would be capable of killing your father?"

"Oh that. I think Sylvia could do it if she wanted to. Mind you, I don't think she did, but she has what it takes to get what she wants."

"Do you think she wanted your father dead?" Latimer treaded carefully.

"I don't know. She's strange sometimes, very cold and unfeeling."

"In his Will your father said she had been hurt. What was that all about?"

"She fell for a man real hard. I mean, she was totally in love and gave him everything. She even put her money in both of their names and he cleaned her out and took off the day before they were supposed to get married. She never got over it. My father told her he was no good, but she didn't listen to him. She had a nervous breakdown and was in an institution for a while. When she got out, she had no money, and my father decided to give her a monthly allowance from then on. He didn't trust her with money anymore." Becky took another sip of coffee and went on. "That's why I think she would kill him, to become independent again." She looked at Latimer with a strange satisfaction. "I don't trust men that much." There was a touch of hardness in her voice, in spite of the giggle.

"Have you been married, Becky?"

"No, and I don't think I ever will. Like I just said, I don't trust men enough. Especially if I come into fifty million dollars, there's no way I would ever dare bind myself to a man so he can take it from me." She got up and stretched out her hand. Her face was lit up by a big smile. "I have an appointment, Mr. Latimer. It was nice to talk to you."

"Thank you for your time, Becky. It has been very helpful." Rachel showed him out. He was absolutely certain she had no appointment in this kind of weather.

His condo was just two blocks down the road. The rain was still coming down in sheets, driven by strong gusts. Glenda was already home and greeted him at the door. She wore an apron over her woolen pants and matching sweater.

"Come on in, you poor thing. It's terrible out there. I started a fire in the fireplace and we're having lasagna and a salad." She kissed him. "I'm so glad you made it home alright, honey."

"I was just down the road at Rebecca Hellman's condo. That was quite an interview. I'll tell you after I've taken a hot shower to warm up."

The fireplace felt great and Latimer huddled in his favorite chair under a blanket. Glenda handed him a cup of hot tea and a small plate of crackers and cheese.

"This is great, sweetheart. Thanks. It has been quite a day. How was yours?"

"Cassie wants us to go to the company event in honor of her wedding. She said she talked to you."

"She did and I left it up to you." Latimer took a sip of tea.

"Does that mean you don't want to go?" Glenda asked.

"I'm like Jerry in that regard. I don't like to get all dressed up and stand around and talk to people I don't know, about things I'm not the least bit interested in."

"She feels very nervous about Jerry. I think there's talk about him already, that he is nothing but a fortune hunter. I think it would be good if we could be there for moral support. If not for Cassie, we could do it for Jerry. He won't know a soul there." Glenda sat by the fireplace on the hearth.

"If you put it that way, I suppose we have to go." He groaned.

"Now tell me what happened today?" Glenda asked.

He told her about the stop at the coroner's office and the shipment of Hellman's blood sample.

"Patricia Hellman was next on my agenda. She is a gracious, sweet lady. Her house and grounds are much bigger than Cassie's. I would love to see it in the summer. She spoiled her children against her husband's wishes and was upset about the terms of the Will." He took another cracker and cheese. "It was my interview with Rebecca Hellman that was interesting. She looks gorgeous in every way, but acts like a ditsy blonde. However, I have a feeling underneath all that is a woman of steel. I would not want to cross her. She definitely had her father fooled."

"What makes you say that?" Glenda asked.

"She was talking about the men in her life. Her father thought she was taken in by them, but he could not have been further from the truth. I have a feeling she uses men for her purposes and then lets them go." He finished his tea. "Can I have another cup? It really helps me to get warm." He got up and stoked the fire as Glenda got the tea.

"Here you are. Dinner will be ready in a few minutes," she said as she handed him the cup.

"The most interesting part of the interview was Becky's assessment about her sister Sylvia. She indicated Sylvia was short on funds, since she gave them over to a man who ran off with her money the day before they were to get married. Apparently, she ended up in a mental institution for a while. Her father kept her on a short leash, financially speaking, since then."

"She would definitely have a motive?" Glenda asked.

"You are right. I still have to interview her."

Dinner was delicious and they spent a cozy evening, sipping tea by the fireplace.

Chapter 4

The next morning the rain had stopped. It had been replaced with a clear sky and freezing temperatures. Latimer arrived at his office a little after nine. Sue Ellen had his coffee ready when he walked in.

"Latimer darlin', it's colder than a coon without fur during a freezing spell in Georgia."

He laughed.

"It doesn't get this cold in Adell, does it, Sue Ellen?"

"No way, it makes me want to go home, where the people are as warm as the weather." She sighed deeply.

"Did you get an appointment for me with the lawyer this morning?"

"I did. It's at nine. You have thirty minutes to get there. I need the tape from your interview yesterday."

"I have it right here." He handed it to her.

"I'll have that done by the time you get back. I'm getting good at transcribing."

Latimer was on the road to Gary Norton's office. The cold wind penetrated his heavy coat and made him shiver as he got out of the car. A fleeting thought of retirement in Florida went through his mind, as he walked up to the three-story, gray building. The legal firm of Norton, Bradshaw and Holloway was on the second floor. A young secretary greeted him with a friendly smile and notified Mr. Norton of his arrival.

"How good to see you again, Mr. Latimer," Gary Norton said as he entered. "How are things going with the investigation?"

"I'm still trying to get everyone to talk to me, as you can imagine," he said and took a seat in front of the lawyer's desk. "I hope you don't mind if I tape our conversation. It helps me not to miss anything I might need later."

"Of course, help yourself."

Latimer prepared the recorder.

"Mr. Norton, what can you tell me about William Carl Hellman?"

"He was a first rate, savvy stock broker and investor for many years. You can tell by the fortune he amassed over the years. He was also a very generous man, who gave large amounts to various charities. His favorite ones, among many others, were the poor and homeless, clinics and hospitals and the church. He was a very religious man who lived what he believed in, at least in this particular area of his life. The only people he did not treat generously were his children. He was actually quite put out with them. In his opinion, they lived off of his money without trying to make it on their own. In spite of unlimited funds, none of them, except the two oldest sons, went to college or worked in a profession of any kind. It greatly disturbed him that he had not been able to instill a better work ethic in his children. I think he blamed his wife for most of it."

"What about his children? Do you think any of them are capable of murdering their father?" Latimer asked.

"Personally, all of them are. They all had a grudge against him for being tight with his money towards them, while giving freely to charity. From what I could gather, it was a very contentious family atmosphere, the older they got."

"What do you think made him think one of them killed him?"

"I truly don't know. He wouldn't or couldn't tell me."

"Was there any sign of unusual illness or behavior when you talked to him during the drawing up of the Will?" Latimer asked.

"All I saw was, that he was extremely tired, even resigned on some days. At other times he was angry. In spite of this, he never seemed to fear death. He strongly believed he knew where he was going. His greatest concern, and maybe the reason for his depression, was that his children did not believe like he did."

"Did he ever talk to them about his faith?"

"Oh yes. That was another area of contention. None of them wanted to have anything to do with religion, including his wife." Gary Norton looked at Latimer with sadness in his eyes.

"If you could pick one, Mr. Norton, which of the children would you say is the most likely suspect?"

"I would think, and this is only speculation mind you, Allan, the youngest, is spoiled enough not to want to wait until the old man died of natural causes." He moved uneasy in his chair. "As a lawyer, I should not be talking like this. It is, however, important to me that you solve the case. Mr. Hellman and I were good friends and I want you to find his murderer." He sounded determined.

"I'm in the process of sending Mr. Hellman's blood sample to an Anscott Research facility in New York to be tested for unusual poisons. This will take a while. I know the owner, and she has agreed to expedite the testing since they normally don't deal with the public. I do expect the Hellman estate to pay for this process."

"Of course Mr. Latimer, I will see to it personally if you submit a bill to my office." Gary Norton sounded excited. "That is the best idea anyone has come up with so far." He got up and walked around his desk. "I'm afraid I have another appointment in five minutes. Let me know how things are going."

On the way out, Latimer was astounded how honest the man had been. As a lawyer, he didn't mince words when it came to the guilt or innocence of the siblings.

It was too early for the appointment with Dr. William Hellman. He went back to his office and dropped off the tape of the interview with Sue Ellen.

"I wouldn't want you to get bored," he said with a grin when he laid it on her desk.

"Mrs. Hellman called. She wants you to stop by her house as soon as you can," Sue Ellen said. "She sounded upset."

"Did she say what it was about?"

"No, but she said it was important."

"I sure hate going out in that cold again," Latimer said on his way out the door. "I won't be back till later this afternoon. I'll go from there to see the good Doctor." He shivered when he got into his car. It was getting colder.

Instead of getting out of the car to ring the button at the gate to the estate, he called and soon it opened. The butler greeted him at the front door.

"Mrs. Hellman is waiting for you, Sir."

"Mr. Latimer, how good of you to come right away." Patricia Hellman looked upset.

"I'm at a loss for words." She was wringing her hands in a dramatic way. "Someone broke into this house and went through my husband's room."

"Have you called the police, Ma'am?" Latimer asked.

"People in my position don't call the police, Mr. Latimer. It would cause unnecessary publicity. I want you to find out what's going on."

"Was anything stolen?" He looked puzzled.

"I can't see that anything is missing. Someone was looking for something. I don't think they found it."

"What makes you think that?"

"I don't know, why else would they mess up William's room?" She sounded vague somehow.

"Can I take a look at the room, Mrs. Hellman?"

"Of course, I've left it the way I found it," she said as she led the way up the big staircase. "William and I had separate rooms. He liked to read late and I like to watch TV in the evening."

Latimer walked into the large bedroom. A huge poster bed dominated the room. The drawers of the two chest-of-drawers were pulled open and the contents strewn on the floor. The bed covers were pulled back with the sheets pulled off the bed. Clothes had been removed from the big walk-in closet and thrown across the room. The two night stands were moved away from the bed with the drawers open. The room looked like a tornado had hit it. The heavy curtains of the two large windows were drawn half way. In the fireplace Latimer noticed fresh ashes as if some papers had been burned recently.

He looked at the mess and couldn't help but feel it had been staged. He didn't know why, it was just a strange feeling. Over the last thirty years as a detective, he had developed a sixth sense for these things. Something wasn't right here, but he couldn't put his finger on it.

"When did you find this mess?" He asked Patricia Hellman.

"It was this morning when the maid came in to dust." She sounded upset.

"When was the last time you had been in here?"

"Yesterday, when Allan came over and wanted to see the room. I don't know why. I thought he just wanted to say goodbye to his father by looking at the room." She dabbed her eyes. "The poor boy was so upset."

"Has anyone else been in here since then?"

"I wouldn't know. It's a big house and we have many servants. Any one of them could have done this." She looked at Latimer with a look of despair. "I don't know how much more I can take. The children are all so upset about this ridiculous Will. Allan nearly had a breakdown yesterday. The poor child really isn't coping well with this."

"How old is Allan?"

"He is twenty-five and a very delicate boy. My husband never appreciated his sensitivities to cope with everyday life." She sniffled into her tissue.

"Is he ill?"

"No, but his nerves get rattled when anything goes wrong. He is such a dear, sweet boy. I have always had to take special care of him and shield him from life's hard realities."

Latimer remembered the video of the Will. Now he understood what William Hellman was talking about, when he said his wife had spoiled the young man to the point he couldn't cope with life.

He stood and looked at the room, deep in thought. What could it be, someone was trying to hide before he could find it? He was sure Patricia had told the children he was coming over this morning. He looked at his watch. It was time for his appointment with William Hellman, the doctor.

"I have to go now, Mrs. Hellman. I have an appointment with your son William at noon, and I have thirty minutes to get to his office. Please, leave the room the way it is. I'll come back when I can and check it out further."

The offices of William Carl Hellman, MD, a Neurosurgeon, were on the second floor of a large medical building. Latimer got there on time and was admitted to see Dr. Hellman fifteen minutes later. He was a handsome, tall man with a strong, masculine face. His perfunctory smile never reached his steel blue eyes. His full, dark brown hair was slightly gray on the sides. He walked around his large desk and shook Latimer's hand and then pointed to one of the heavy leather chairs, while he sat in the other.

"This is very awkward for me, Mr. Latimer. To be accused of murdering my father is not what I ever expected to experience. However, I know this is not your fault. Let's get on with it then, I don't have much time." His tone was short, but professional.

"I should let you know I'm as surprised by this as you are, Doctor. Do you mind if I tape our conversation? It helps me keep my information straight."

"Certainly."

"How was your relationship with your father, Sir? I noticed on the video he was quite proud of you, the only one of his children. That must've made you feel good."

"My father and I didn't have much to say to each other. I never realized he approved of what I was doing. To criticize my family life really ticked me off, to tell you the truth. Like he mentioned, he was not exactly Father of the Year. The crazy Will confirms it. To suggest any one of us killed him, is ludicrous."

"You may appreciate that I have sent off a blood sample of your father's to an Anscott Research facility to be analyzed for a poison, which causes heart failure without leaving a trace."

"I don't know of such a thing, but there are some exotic poisons who might qualify. It would take quite a search to find it, though." He was thinking. "You really think one of us did kill him then?"

"I have no idea, Dr. Hellman. If you had your pick, which of your siblings do you think would be capable of doing this?" Latimer asked, not expecting much of an answer.

"I have no idea. I don't need his money. I make enough on my own. Neither did I hate him. It's just we weren't close."

"What about Sylvia, she was the only one who didn't have any money and would be happy to get fifty million," Latimer suggested.

"I hate to speak ill of my sister, Mr. Latimer, but she would have what it takes to pull this off. Her relationship with my father was tenuous at best." He leaned back in his chair. "My father was a very nice, kindhearted man. He just didn't know how to relate to his children."

"Was he a good husband?"

"They fought a lot about how to treat the children. My mother is overindulgent and he was too strict. You can imagine the turmoil that caused in their marriage." He stroked his face. "I can't say I'm all that much better with my wife and kids. My father did have a point when he said I should spend more time with my family."

"Dr. Hellman, you've been most helpful. Thank you. I hope I can call on you again should the need arise?" Latimer turned the recorder off and got up.

"I will be glad to talk to you again, Mr. Latimer. I really want this thing to be over with, so we can all get on with our lives." He shook Latimer's hand and showed him out.

Latimer was impressed with the man.

Chapter 5

Wednesday morning Latimer went directly from home to Sylvia Hellman's condo. It was on the other side of town and it took him forty minutes to get to the high-rise on the eastside of Glenridge. It was situated in the middle of a small park. The complex had three tall buildings made up entirely of condominiums. Her apartment was on the seventh floor of the one in the middle.

The doorman had been notified and let Latimer in without asking many questions. He had a feeling her father must've paid for this place, because everything he saw was plush and state of the art.

A woman in her mid-thirties answered the door. She was petite with dark, thick hair hanging to her shoulders. Her small, blue eyes looked cold. She wore jeans and an expensive sweater. Her outfit showed off a trim, curvy figure.

"Come in, Mr. Latimer. I've been expecting you." She looked at him with apprehension and disapproval. "I hope you understand I resent this whole thing. Another one of my father's religious antics I suppose."

Latimer walked in after her into a large living room with a breathtaking view over the park. It was furnished with contemporary, expensive looking, solid oak furniture. A couch sat facing the large windows with two comfortable chairs to match. She pointed to one of them and took a seat on the couch.

"Well, I don't see the point of this interview, but I guess you don't really have a choice in this matter either, do you?" Her tone was icy. She did not offer him coffee or any other refreshments. Her entire demeanor showed open hostility.

"I hope you don't mind if I turn the recorder on. It helps me remember." He had a twinkle in his eyes as he continued. "At my age, I need all the help I can get."

"My father would've never hired you if you were a senile, old man, Mr. Latimer. So let's get down to business without it."

Latimer stuck the recorder back into his coat pocket without a word.

"Can you tell me about your relationship with your father, Ms. Hellman?"

"What's there to tell? I hated him and he thought I was a mindless fool."

"That is not what he said on the video I heard." Latimer said.

"I don't care what he said. He would've never cut me off if he had not thought I would squander my money again on worthless people." Her voice was hard.

"Can you tell me if you visited him often when he got sick?"

"I went to see my mother, but I never saw him. We would've just argued, as usual. So what's the point?" She made a flippant motion with her hand.

"Do you have a good relationship with your mother?"

"Yes. She is the one who helped all of us when Father would go on about his favorite subject of not giving us money, because he wanted us to make it on our own. I guess it made him feel better to see me grovel for it, but I never did. I got along just fine without his pitiful allowance."

"What did you do to make money, Ms. Hellman?" Latimer asked carefully.

"That is none of your business. Let's just say, I'm doing well as you can see." She pointed to the rest of the apartment."

"If you could guess, which one of your siblings do you think would be capable of killing your father?" He held his breath.

"I don't think any of them have the guts to do it, or the brains, except my brother William. But he is way too stuffy and unimaginative to come up with it. Besides, he makes plenty on his own. He's the only one who doesn't have to care how the Will turns out." There was tension in her voice as she spoke.

"You are the only one who could use the fifty million, the way I understand it." He knew he was on dangerous ground.

"Are you insinuating I killed him? You have a nerve to come here and accuse me. I think you better leave. I may not have liked my father, but I would never stoop so low as to kill him." She was standing over Latimer. "Get out of my house. I've had enough of all these ridiculous questions. I never want to see you again." She was shouting by now.

Latimer raised himself up to his full height and looked down on her with a cold smile. "Me thinks ye protest too much, Ms. Hellman." He bowed slightly and walked out.

As Brighton would say, 'That went well'. Latimer reached into his coat pocket and turned the recorder off. He grinned. He was no longer an Inspector. He could afford to do these things now without getting into trouble.

He turned his cell phone back on when he sat down in the car. It rang immediately. It was Sue Ellen.

"Latimer darlin', the Hellman's butler called. He wants to talk to you."

"Does he want me to meet him at the estate?" Latimer asked.

"No, he's here at the office. I told him you'd be back in a few minutes."

"I just got done with the interview. It'll be thirty minutes before I can make it back to the office. Ask him if he wants to wait or come back."

"He says he'd rather wait."

"Ok, I'll try to hurry." Latimer was intrigued. What could the butler want to tell him that he didn't dare say at the estate?

It took a little longer to make it because of traffic, but Henry Gossomer was still waiting when Latimer got back. He looked upset and tense.

"Please come into my office. Sue Ellen, could you get us a cup of coffee, please?"

After she brought the coffee, Latimer pointed to the chairs in front of his desk. They both took a seat.

"What is it you want to talk to me about, Henry?"

"I am very uncomfortable doing this, Mr. Latimer. I've been with the Hellman family for a long time. I feel like a traitor talking about them in a negative way, but my loyalties were with Mr. Hellman. He was a good man and tried to raise his children right. It was his wife who turned them into the, how shall I put it, spoiled, lazy people they are." He shifted uneasy in his seat. "I am sorry to put it so bluntly, but it is the only way to describe them."

"Even Dr. Hellman?" Latimer asked.

"He is not as bad, but he lets his wife and children do the taking." Henry was clearly upset by now.

"What is it you came to tell me, Henry?" Latimer's voice was gentle.

"You remember, Mrs. Hellman called you to look at the Mr. Hellman's bedroom? She said some of the staff might have done it. I know better. It was her. I saw her coming out of the room late the night before. I couldn't sleep and got up to get me some milk to take my medicine."

"Are you saying Mrs. Hellman messed up the room?"

"Yes, she was out of breath when I saw her come out on the landing. She looked around to see if anyone had seen her and then went to her room. I was standing in the shadow and she didn't see me. After I took my medicine, I snuck upstairs and checked Mr. Hellman's bedroom. It was messed up and there were some glowing ashes in the fireplace." He sighed. "I can't imagine why she would do that. If I could guess, it's to protect one of the children. There must've been something in that room they didn't want you to find, Mr. Latimer."

"Are you saying one of the children murdered Mr. Hellman and his wife knows who did it?" Latimer was incredulous.

"That's the only explanation I can find for her behavior," Henry said as he twisted a tissue in his hands. "I'm so sorry to have to say it. She is not always the sweet lady she pretends to be and would do anything for her children."

"That definitely puts a new spin on this case, Henry. I will certainly take into consideration what you told me. However, things aren't always what they seem. As I unravel this case, this might not mean what you think, and there maybe an innocent explanation." He tried to calm the butler's nerves. "I appreciate you coming to me. Please, keep your eyes and ears open and let me know if you see anything else out of the ordinary." Latimer got up. "Thank you so much for coming by, Henry." He followed him to the front door. "Before you go, do you have your own cell phone number I could call if I need to?"

"Yes, I do."

"Please give it to Sue Ellen. She will give you mine. That way we can have a private conversation if it should become necessary." They exchanged numbers and Henry left.

"Sue Ellen, why don't you order us a pizza, I'm paying."

"With all that money you're getting for this case, I should think so, Latimer darlin'." She grinned. "When are you getting a filing cabinet and a new desk for me?"

"Let's just do the pizza today." He laughed. "You go on line and order whatever you think you need. Just don't spend all my money."

"This is better than a flea jumping on a dog," she said in her most lilting Georgia drawl.

The temperature was well below freezing as he got into his car to drive to the Hellman estate. It didn't feel like it had warmed up, even by afternoon. He was curious about Allan Hellman, since he had heard so much about him from the video and his mother. He was ready to pull the same stunt with the recorder if the man didn't agree to the recording of the interview. Latimer wondered if he should bother looking at the bedroom again, since he was sure whatever there had been was gone. He even doubted there ever had been anything at all, and wondered why the ruse?

Henry let him in the house when he got there.

"Please, come in, Mr. Latimer. Mr. Allan and Mrs. Hellman are waiting for you." He led Latimer into the same room to the left as before.

"Mr. Latimer is here to see you, Madam."

"Please, come in, Mr. Latimer, how good to see you again." Patricia Hellman greeted him with a warm smile. "This is my son Allan." She pointed to a young man of slight build and almost delicate features. He was no taller than his mother and had dark, short hair, brown eyes and a slender nose. He very much resembled her. He was dressed in jeans and a heavy sweater. His lips seemed to be in a perpetual pout. His eyes were cast down as if he didn't dare look up as Latimer walked toward him. He remained in his chair and didn't make any move to get up or shake his hand.

"I know I have to talk to you, Mr. Latimer, but I don't have to like it." His voice was thin and without strength. "I'm really mad about this. So, ask your questions and be done with it." There was a hint of petulance in his tone.

"Thank you for your time, Mr. Hellman," Latimer said as he pulled his recorder out of his pocket. "I hope you don't mind if I record our conversation?"

"Why would you want to do that, so you can use it in court?"

"No, of course not, this is to help me remember what was said." He tried the old age trick again. "At my age I need all the help I can get."

"Ok. It's alright, I guess."

Latimer sat down in the chair closest to Allan.

"Tell me about your relationship with your father." He asked.

"You heard the old man on the video. He hated my guts and thought I was useless. What else can I say?" I didn't care that much about him either." He sounded angry.

"Try to be nice, Allan, dear," Patricia Hellman said. "We don't need to share everything about our family affairs."

"Mother, he already heard it from Father. There's nothing to hide. The old man held his money like a carrot in front of me and never gave me enough to do what I want." He didn't turn to his mother when he spoke.

"What was it you wanted that he wouldn't give you, Allan? May I call you Allan?" Latimer asked.

"Sure." He waved his hand in a dismissive gesture. "My father was the stingiest man in the world. With all the money he had, he wanted me to go to school and then get a job." He pointed toward himself. "Do I look like a regular working stiff to you, Mr. Latimer?"

Latimer smiled at him with a non-committal smile.

"I don't know what a regular working stiff looks like, Allan. If you think about it, your father worked every day and so does your brother."

"I would think you're one of them, aren't you?" He looked at him defiantly.

"I guess you could say that." Latimer leaned back in his comfortable chair. "Tell me something, what will you do if this working stiff doesn't solve this case and you don't get your fifty million for ten years, son?" Latimer pointed to himself.

Allan looked at him, totally stunned.

"I hadn't thought of that." He shifted in his seat. "I'm sorry, Mr. Latimer, I didn't mean to be rude." He suddenly looked like a little boy who got caught doing something bad. "I just want what's mine."

"Allan, did you visit your father every day when he was sick?" Latimer asked.

"I made him do it, Mr. Latimer," Patricia answered instead. "He didn't want to, but I thought it was the right thing to do."

"I didn't care," Allan said. "He just lay in bed and didn't say much, other than his religious stuff I didn't want to hear. I told him and after a while he quit talking to me altogether. He got too sick, I guess."

"Did that upset you in any way to see him get more ill every day?" Latimer asked.

"Not really. I knew he was dying and there was nothing I could do about it." His tone was almost detached. "We all got to go sometime."

"Can you tell me, if you have any idea, which one of your siblings might have killed your father?" Latimer went on.

"I don't know." He looked up as if thinking hard. "I think Grant is wild and has the courage to do something like that. He was always broke and came to Mom for money all the time. He told me once he wished Father would either give him some more or die so he could inherit."

"When was that?" Latimer asked.

"A long time ago, I think, maybe three or four years."

"Did you ever wish he was dead for the same reason, Allan?"

"I didn't care. Mom always gave me money when I needed it." He looked at her and smiled. "She's really great that way. That's why I don't really care how long it takes, because he left her enough to keep us all going."

Latimer reached for the recorder on the table. He was ready to quit. This kid really got to him. He tried hard to keep his disgust hidden. At this moment he was glad he didn't have children.

"Thank you for your time, Allan. You've been helpful. Thank you, Mrs. Hellman." He got up. "Do you think I could look at your husband's bedroom again?"

"Of course Mr. Latimer, Henry will show you the way." She pushed a button on the coffee table and Henry appeared in the door.

"Do you see anything missing, Henry?" Latimer asked when they were in the bedroom.

"It's hard to tell with all this mess, Sir. On the surface, I don't see anything. I will check more thoroughly when I straighten things out. Maybe then I can tell you more."

Latimer walked around slowly. It was a masculine bedroom with heavy, dark furniture and bedcover. There was no sign that Patricia Hellman had ever spent any time in here. He opened an ornate box on one of the dressers. It was filled with a man's jewelry. There was a Rolex watch and several gold rings, old fashioned cufflinks and a wedding ring. He picked up a gold tie clasp with a large diamond on it.

It definitely wasn't robbery, Latimer thought. This stuff was worth a fortune.

"Let me know if you find anything missing, Henry. I would appreciate it."

"I will go over everything carefully, Sir," Henry said as they left to go downstairs.

His cell phone rang on his way home. It was Glenda.

"I just faxed a letter to the coroner from Cassie, ordering the tests. She called the Anscott Research Laboratories and they told her it would take two weeks to do the testing. The coroner needs to specify in detail what the objective is and the kind of poisons to look for. You need to talk to her and tell her exactly what you suspect as well. Also, make sure they have the address of Mr. Norton for the bill."

"That sounds wonderful, Glenda. Please tell Cassie thank you and that I owe her. I'm on my way home. Do you want me to get take-out?"

"That would be nice. This weekend we need to get something for both of us to wear to the company event for Cassie and Jerry." Glenda said.

"My one and only black suit won't do?" He asked in mock horror.

"No, it won't. I will not have you go and stick out like a sore thumb. We're Cassie's close friends and can't put her to shame. She'll have enough trouble getting Jerry accepted by the company VIP's. You have no idea what a snobbish crowd that can be. Andrea and I are going with her and Jerry all day tomorrow to pick out something to wear." Glenda sounded excited.

"Maybe you can find something for you at the same time?" he asked, hoping he wouldn't have to go with her on Saturday.

"Those places will be slightly out of my league, honey. We're flying to New York on the company jet." She laughed. "It would definitely break our bank account, even with your recent infusion of funds."

"I can just picture Jerry in one of those high-end stores, trying on clothes. It will be interesting. If he can survive that, he can handle anything." Latimer was laughing.

"I have to go, see you at home," Glenda said. "Goodbye."

He had forgotten about the event. It would be in less than two weeks. He groaned. He was not looking forward to it, and could only imagine what pressure this would be on Jerry. He dialed his number.

"Jerry, this is Latimer. How are you doing?"

"Latimer, I'm glad you called. I wish you would come with me to New York tomorrow. I've already asked Peter and he won't go. He says he hates that kind of thing." Jerry sounded desperate.

"Jerry, you're a good friend and all that, but you're asking me to do something I wouldn't even do for my dying mother." Latimer was laughing. "I was thinking before I called you, if you can handle that ordeal, you can handle anything."

"Ordeal is the perfect word for this. The ladies are all excited. I told Cassie just to get me a suit and bring it back with her and I'll wear anything she picks out. She wouldn't go for it. I have to try it on. We had our first fight about it." He groaned. "Latimer, I need moral support. Please, come with me."

"You're on you own, buddy. It's enough I have to go to that big company shindig in two weeks. Glenda is dragging me to buy my own suit this coming Saturday. There's no way I can do this twice. Why don't you ask your Mom or your sister?"

"Are you crazy, another woman? No way, I need a man to keep me sane," Jerry shouted.

"Listen Jerry, I just called to give you my condolences on your trip tomorrow. "This too shall pass, my friend."

In spite of his light hearted tone, he was worried about Jerry. He wondered if all this wasn't putting a strain on their marriage. The man truly was not prepared for this kind of corporate social life. Cassie grew up with it and felt comfortable. How would she react if they snubbed Jerry? Surely no one would openly dare, since she was the owner. He hoped he and Glenda could make Jerry feel better.

He picked up Chinese take-out, his favorite. It would feel wonderful to sit in front of the fireplace tonight. The temperatures were falling rapidly. He looked forward to spending a peaceful evening with Glenda.

He called Pat Christianson, the coroner.

"Pat, Glenda just called me to tell you, Cassie Anscott Sanders faxed you the letter you asked for. Make sure you give them some kind of hint what the poison could be so they can narrow down the search.

She also said to include Gary Norton's address to send the bill to him." He gave her the address. "Make sure you send your bill there as well."

"I've been thinking about some possibilities, handsome, but I'm not up on the latest when it comes to exotic poisons. There have been some new ones found in the Amazon jungle, but that is as much as I know," she said. "I will mention that to them."

"I would have no idea how any of the people involved could get a hold of anything like that." Latimer wondered.

"Enough money will get you anything and you can find it on the internet. It isn't that hard anymore these days. Take care, Latimer." She hung up.

Chapter 6

Glenda was late coming home. She looked upset and worried when she walked in the door.

"What's wrong, sweetheart?" He kissed her on the cheek.

"Cassie and Jerry had a fight. He refuses to go tomorrow 'to be dressed like a stuffed turkey', as he put it."

"Is it necessary for him to fly to New York? One suit looks as good as another, and I'm sure he can find one right here in Glenridge." Latimer was careful to sound casual.

"You have no idea about the pressure on Cassie with this. She's the one who will be on display a lot more than Jerry. If he doesn't measure up, she'll be the one laughed and gossiped about." Glenda sounded tense.

The phone rang and Latimer answered it. It was Jerry.

"Latimer, I'm trying hard to deal with this New York thing. Cassie is crying and I don't know what to do. I told her, if you go with me, I'll go. The two of us will go to the store without the women. That's my deal." The silence was deafening while Latimer considered what to do. Suddenly, Cassie was on the phone.

"Bob, if you come with us and do this I would be so grateful. To show you how grateful, you buy whatever suit you want while you two are in the store and I will foot the bill." She sounded desperate.

"Cassie, I'm not a charity case, I can buy my own clothes." Latimer sounded tense.

"I don't mean it that way. You told Jerry you didn't want to go twice to buy something for the party. This way you only have to go once." He could tell she was nearly in tears.

"If it is that important to you, Cassie, I guess I better go with Jerry. But I'll have no interference from you ladies. Whatever Jerry and I buy for him, you'll accept without saying a word." He sighed.

"I promise." She handed the phone to Jerry,

"Thanks, I won't forget. You're a true friend, Bob. I will see you at the airport in the morning."

"I think we've taken those two to raise," Latimer said with slight exasperation in his voice after he hung up.

"Thanks for doing this, honey. You have no idea how much it means to Cassie and me."

"How's this going to work? Do we know which store to go to?" He asked, suddenly realizing, he had no idea where to go.

"I called ahead. They know you're coming. I told them exactly what kind of suit and everything else he'll need. All you two have to do is walk in. Just make sure you go along with what they suggest. Just don't tell Jerry. He'll go along with what you say, I'm sure." She looked a little smug.

"You girls are something else." He shook his head in amazement. "There is nothing women will not stoop down to in order to get us men to do what they want." He looked at Glenda. "Are you getting an outfit as well?"

"No, I wouldn't accept it. Cassie offered, but we're talking thousands of dollars and I can't do that. It's you who is doing her the favor. I'm just doing my job."

They had to get up quite early the next morning. It was bitter cold outside. Since there was hardly any traffic, they reached the corporate airport in record time. It was designed for business traffic with private and corporate jets. Cassie and Jerry weren't there yet. The stewardess asked them to take a seat in the warm interior of the plane. She brought steaming hot coffee for both of them as soon as they sat down.

"Maybe this isn't such a terrible ordeal after all," Latimer mumbled as he took a sip and smiled at Glenda. "Remind me later to call Sue Ellen and tell her I won't be in today." He looked out of the window and saw Cassie and Jerry walk up the steps.

"Hey, there you are," Cassie said with a bright smile when she walked in.

"They must have worked things out between them," Glenda whispered in Latimer's ear.

"You and I are sitting in the back," Jerry said to Latimer. "I need some space away from those scheming women." He was smiling when he said it. "I really appreciate this more than you can ever imagine, Bob," he said when they had settled into their seat a few rows back. The plane was getting ready to take off. "I hope this is not a regular thing. I don't think I could take it, as much as I love Cassie."

He was interrupted by the pilot over the intercom.

"Welcome on board, Mr. and Mrs. Sanders. It looks like we have calm weather and should be in New York in a little more than an hour. The crew wishes you and your guests a pleasant flight."

"You knew it would be an adjustment, Jerry." Latimer went on after the announcement. "Every marriage has its bumps in the beginning. It will get easier. This is not about what you don't like, Jerry. It's all about what you two have together. These small incidents mean absolutely nothing in the long run." Latimer waved to the stewardess to get him some more coffee as soon as they were in the air.

An hour and a half later the plane landed in New York.

"Let the fun begin," Jerry said as he took Cassie's hand. "Remember, no interference."

"I promise." She gave him a kiss and a bright smile. "I love you, baby."

A car was waiting to take them to their designated store.

Latimer and Jerry were sitting in a small restaurant close to the men's store they had just left. A waiter with a French accent brought the menu. Jerry looked at Latimer with a big question mark on his face.

"I have no idea what any of this means, do you?"

"I don't have a clue." Latimer looked at the waiter. "Can you recommend something for us to eat since we don't speak French?"

"My name is Bill for those who want to know what they're getting and Francois to those who don't." He grinned mischievously.

"Now we're getting somewhere," Jerry said. "Do you have anything close to a hamburger and French fries?"

"I would like a steak, baked potato and a salad," Latimer said.

"I can handle that, gentlemen. Would you like some wine?"

"Why not," Jerry said. "Just bring us what you think goes along with the meal."

Before long, each of them had a plate of what they had ordered put in front of them. Bill even mentioned the French name as he put them down. He tried hard to suppress a grin.

"We made it, Latimer," Jerry said as he took a bite out of the fancy hamburger. "I don't understand how that guy in the store knew just what I needed. I didn't really have to say much, did I? That was easier than I thought."

Latimer didn't say a word and kept on eating.

They met the ladies at the plane later in the afternoon. On the flight home Cassie bubbled over with excitement about her dress. She sat next to Jerry and the two held hands and kissed like newlyweds should.

Glenda told Latimer that Cassie insisted on buying her a dress she really liked after all.

"I don't know how much it was. In those kinds of stores they don't do price tags. Cassie made me try it on and it does look gorgeous. We are all well dressed for the big night." She leaned over and kissed Latimer on the cheek. "Thanks for going with us, big guy."

Latimer and Glenda spent a quiet weekend at home. He tried hard not to think about the case as they sat in front of the fireplace, glad not to have to go out into the bitter cold outside.

Chapter 7

Latimer was still at home Monday morning when the call came from Henry Gossomer.

"I need to see you today, Mr. Latimer. It's urgent. I found something in the bedroom. I would have called earlier, but I haven't been feeling well." He sounded weak and spoke in a whisper. "I'm still in bed, unable to get up. Please come before it's too late." The phone went dead.

Latimer dialed back immediately, but it went straight to voice mail. He had just finished his breakfast and rushed into the bedroom where Glenda was getting dressed.

"I have to go to the Hellman estate immediately. Something's wrong with Henry, the butler." He threw on his clothes, kissed Glenda goodbye and left before she could ask any questions. He was impatient when it took a long time for anyone to answer his ring at the gate. One of the maids finally let him in.

"Sir, something terrible has happened," she said when she met him at the front door. "We just found Henry real sick in his bed." She was crying.

"Have you called the ambulance?"

"I don't know. Mrs. Hellman is too upset I think." She took him to the family room in the back. He found Patricia Hellman sobbing. Allan sat next to her and held her hand. He hardly looked up when Latimer entered.

"Have you called the ambulance, Mr. Hellman?"

"No, can't you see we are too upset right now? He's just sick" He sounded insolent.

Latimer dialed 911. While he waited for them to arrive, he asked the maid to show him to Henry's bedroom. The butler lay very still. His face was contorted in pain. Latimer saw tiny bits of saliva around his mouth. Nothing seemed to be disturbed in the room. It looked extremely neat and tidy. It made Latimer wonder if someone had straightened it out or the man was overly meticulous. Latimer walked up to the side of the bed. Something was really wrong here.

"Henry, can you hear me? It's Latimer."

There was no response. His eyes were closed and he was barely breathing.

"Henry, hang in there, the ambulance is on its way. You'll be alright." Latimer took his hand and held it. "I'll stay with you until they get here." He was leaning over to check if the man was still breathing when the EMS crew walked in.

"Step away from the bed, Sir," one of the men said. "Better yet, why don't you let us do our work and leave the room? We'll take care of him."

Latimer did as he was told. At that moment Det. Sgt. Kevin Brighton with the Glenridge Major Crime Unit walked up the stairs.

"It looks like we're going to work together again, Latimer," he said with his usual bright smile. "It seems every time I get a new case, you have something to do with it. Why don't we talk after I'm done here so you can fill me in what you think is going on."

Latimer was impressed how professional and mature the Kid sounded these days. He was glad he didn't call him that anymore. In spite of his youthful and friendly demeanor, Kevin Brighton had become an outstanding detective.

"He's not dead, Brighton, what are you doing here?" he asked him.

"Can you fill me in why you're here this morning, Latimer?" Brighton asked him on the way down. "The Chief called me and said he thought this was related to Mr. Hellman's death. He just wants me to look into it and find out for sure."

"Henry Gossomer called me about an hour ago and pleaded with me to come see him. He said he found something in Mr. Hellman's bedroom." Latimer told him in a nutshell what had transpired. He also mentioned the agreement he had with Henry to let him know if he found anything unusual. Latimer continued on the way down the steps.

"This sounds like attempted murder to me," Brighton said before they entered the family room. "Feel free to ask questions, Latimer."

Patricia Hellman and her son Allan were sitting on the couch. She had stopped crying and looked up at Latimer.

"I can't believe he's gone. I don't know how I'm going to go on without him. He's been a part of my life for over twenty years." She sniffled into a tissue as Brighton introduced himself.

"Can you tell me what happened, Mrs. Hellman?" He asked.

"Henry hadn't been feeling good for two days. Finally, when he didn't come down this morning, I sent Kathy up to see what was wrong. She told me she thought he was dead."

"Did you have family over for the weekend, Mrs. Hellman?" Latimer asked.

"Yes, all my children were here all day Saturday. We discussed the Will for the first time in detail and what to do about it."

"Was your son Grant here as well?" He continued.

"Yes, he came back on Saturday at noon and all of us had dinner together that evening. It was nice to have them all here."

"Did your son's wife come as well?"

"Yes, of course. William's wife Linda and their two children arrived that afternoon and I got to spend some time with them." She was feeling better as she talked. "It cheered me up to play with my grandchildren. It doesn't happen very often."

"Did Henry complain about any specific problem, Mrs. Hellman?" Brighton asked.

"No, he just said he wasn't feeling well."

"When did that start, Ma'am?" he continued.

"Saturday evening, after dinner, he informed me he wasn't well before I went to my room for the night. Since he had Sunday off, I didn't think about it anymore when I didn't see him."

"Had he complained about being ill before this?" Brighton asked.

"Henry was never sick as long as I can remember," she said. "He was a wonderful butler. "I was so glad my husband left him some money for his services."

Brighton turned to Allan.

"How do you feel about all this?"

"He has been here as long as I can remember. I never paid much attention to him as long as he did what I asked him to do. I know nothing about his private life and I really can't say that I care." He looked at Brighton as if he was bored by all this.

"Can you think of anyone who would want him dead?" Latimer asked quietly.

"You've got to be kidding? Who would want to kill a butler? The man wasn't worth the trouble. He was just a servant."

Latimer didn't try to hide his disgust when he looked at Allan.

"You're all heart, aren't you, son?"

"Allan doesn't mean it that way, Mr. Latimer. Things don't always come out right when he talks to people he doesn't know very well. He's really a good boy at heart." She took Allan's hand in a protective gesture.

"If you say so, Ma'am," Latimer said without taking his eyes off Allan. The young man shrank into the cushion of the couch and looked down, clinging to his mother's hand.

"By the way, Mrs. Hellman, Henry is not dead. He is unconscious and will be taken to the hospital immediately," Brighton said in a calm tone.

Latimer watched carefully for a reaction. Allan looked astonished and slightly annoyed. There was a hint of fear in his eyes, but he could be mistaken.

"Oh, that is wonderful, Mr. Latimer. Maybe he will be ok." Mrs. Hellman looked genuinely glad and stopped crying. "I hope they'll do everything they can to help him get better."

One of the EMS guys stood in the door.

"I would like to talk to you, Det. Sgt. Brighton."

"Come with me, Latimer," Brighton said. The two of them followed the man down the hall toward the front door.

"This definitely looks like attempted murder to me. The saliva around the mouth, the signs of pain on his facial features and the slight discoloration under the finger nails point to poison. The ER doctor told us to draw some blood." He stepped aside as they carried the butler out to the ambulance parked at the front door.

We need to send a sample to Anscott Research Laboratories, Brighton," Latimer said. "Why should we do all the work when they are in the process already? If I'm not mistaken, there's no lab qualified to test for it here in Glenridge."

"I think the Chief gave me this case because he knows you're part of this. It worked so well the last time, why break up a good team, huh?" Brighton smiled. "I'm glad."

"Let's hope we do as well this time, Det. Sergeant." He looked at Brighton. "Although I know you can very well handle this yourself."

"It makes me feel better to have you here, Latimer. I guess I'm not quite ready to cut the strings yet. Also, it feels good to work with you again." He waved goodbye as he got into his car.

On the way to his office, Latimer had time to think about the butler's illness. Henry had tried to do the right thing. Latimer wondered which one of the children tried to kill him. Since every one of them had been there on Saturday, there was no telling. It really would've helped if he knew what Henry had tried to tell him. Now, all he could hope was, he would live to tell him.

It was noon. He took out his cell phone and called to see if Glenda wanted to have lunch with him.

"I'm sorry, honey, I can't today. With all the days I missed, I'm swamped with work. Cassie is gone to a meeting and I have to hold down the fort. I'll see you tonight. On second thought, maybe we can go out for dinner? Why don't I meet you at The Seven Seas and we'll have seafood? We haven't been there in a while."

"That sounds good, how about at six?"

"Great, see you then." She hung up.

Latimer called Sue Ellen to make an appointment with Grant Hellman, now that he was back in town.

"I'm way ahead of you, Latimer, darlin'. You're to see him at his place at two this afternoon. It's in the same high rise as his sister Rebecca's."

"Thanks, Sue Ellen, you're great."

"Does that mean I get a raise?" She was laughing.

"After all the new stuff you're going to buy for the office, I can't afford it, girl," he said with a chuckle and hung up.

By the time he stopped for lunch, he would have just enough time to make it to the other side of the city. He pulled into a Mister Burger and had one of those unhealthy meals he wouldn't tell Glenda about. She was a stickler for healthy food. He definitely wouldn't make it today with two meals out and asked for a hamburger without mayonnaise or French fries. It didn't feel like he was cheating this way.

When he drove up to the condo building, the sun had gone behind dark clouds. It felt like snow. Grant Hellman's condo was on the third floor. Another ungrateful brat, he thought as he knocked on the door.

"It opened almost immediately. He looked at a tall, handsome man in his late thirties with full, dark hair, a short beard and a trim athletic figure. His piercing, blue eyes looked at Latimer with amusement.

"Ah, here comes the detective who is going to get me my fifty million dollars if I answer all his questions." He waved Latimer in with a dramatic gesture. "Come on in and ask away and see if I did it." He had a big, friendly grin on his face. "I'm Grant, Mr. Latimer. Welcome to my man cave, where women are allowed to visit, but do not stay."

Latimer liked this guy immediately.

"Thank you for seeing me, Mr. Hellman."

"It's Grant, please. Mr. Hellman was good old Dad." He pointed to a big, comfortable seating area in front of the big window. The condo had the same lay-out as Rebecca's. Where hers was light and airy, his was filled with dark, heavy furniture. It was definitely masculine, yet with an air of elegance. Latimer noted it was neat and clean. A picture of the entire family was prominently displayed on one of the book shelves along the wall.

"There they all are, Mr. Latimer, my illustrious family. Don't they look nice? Imagine, one of them killed my dad. It's hard to imagine." He suddenly sounded serious. He pointed to one of the chairs. Please, have a seat. Can I bring you some coffee? I just made a fresh pot."

"Thank you. That would be nice, and call me Latimer. Everybody does."

"Great, Latimer. Here is your coffee," he said as he put it on the coffee table. "Now then, what would you like to know?"

"Is it ok if I tape our conversation?" It helps this old brain remember." Latimer used the familiar line.

"I don't think for one minute you need any help in that area, Latimer," Grant Hellman said with a smile. "Go ahead, I don't mind at all."

"It seems to me, you didn't dislike your father as much as the others?" Latimer said as he took a sip.

"I don't really dislike anyone, Latimer. My old man was a kind, generous guy with a big heart toward the poor. I don't blame him for being upset with all of us for not working." He pointed to himself. "Me included. For the first time in my life I realized that, was when I heard his video. I did go to college, but never finished my Masters or applied my business degree in anything worth mentioning." He looked at Latimer with a touch of sadness. "I want to change that. My dad's words really stung me to the point I want to make it up to him." He leaned forward. "I have a feeling I'm the only one who loved him and that includes my mom. All she wanted was to give his money to her lazy kids."

"Your brother William doesn't strike me as lazy, Grant."

"You're right. He isn't, but he didn't get along with Dad whatsoever. I don't think the two ever said two words to each other as long as I can remember."

"How about you, did you talk to him much?" Latimer asked.

"I did more than the others, but he was gone a lot when I was growing up. We had some nice talks later on, but by that time, it was hard because of my wild antics."

"Was that to get his attention?"

"Are you sure you're not a shrink, Latimer?" He laughed in a pleasant manner. "Looking back, that's probably true."

"There is still plenty of time to make it up to him, you know?" Latimer said as he looked at him with smile. "You can still finish your Masters degree and start a business with the money you will inherit, unless of course you killed him." He looked him straight in the eyes.

"So much for the shrink theory, you really don't pull any punches, do you?" He was still smiling. "I didn't kill him. Unlike my siblings, I never wanted to either."

"That is an astounding thing to say, Grant. What makes you think they all wanted to?"

"Every one of them was angry, because he didn't give them enough money to blow. He wasn't tight with money at all. I understood what he was doing. He desired for us to make something of ourselves and make it on our own. His Will proved he wanted to share his wealth with all of us, just not until we were ready." He looked intense.

"Why then did you live exactly like the others?" Your father mentioned a new car every six months." Latimer asked.

"I don't know, a car doesn't really mean that much to me." He sounded irritated. "I'm going to change that. I've had enough of being a useless man with no goal or purpose. Like I said, Latimer, that video really got to me."

"I'm going to be frank, Grant. I thought I came here to talk to another spoiled brat today and found a young man, wanting to change his life. I hope you can pull it off." Latimer leaned forward to put his cup down. "I have one more question. Which one of your siblings is the most likely to have murdered your father?"

"I have thought about that a great deal. I think my youngest brother Allan is spoiled enough to do it. Does he have the brains? I don't know. The girls definitely don't. Maybe Sylvia, but Becky is a ditsy blonde and wouldn't know a brain if it hit her head on. My bet is on Allan. He's a weak person, spoiled and pampered by my mother. His type will go to any length to get what he wants and then goes ballistic when he doesn't get it."

"Did you know Henry Gossomer, the butler, was found poisoned in his bed this morning?" Latimer said in a soft voice.

"What? Henry is dead? What was wrong with him?" He sounded totally surprised.

"He's not dead, but apparently he was poisoned."

Grant looked at Latimer with a look of horror.

"He is a faithful, kind man, who gave his whole life in service to my family." Anger swept over his face. "I loved that man. He would help me when my dad didn't have time to show me how to solve my math problems in school. He even took me fishing sometimes by the lake in back of our house." He had tears in his eyes. "This hits me as hard as my father's death. He was like a stand-in for my dad many times. He and I were the only ones close among my brothers and sisters. They treated him like a servant. He was a friend to me." He was visibly shaken.

"It happened when all of you were at the house this past Saturday." Latimer said. "He called me this morning to tell me he found something in your father's bedroom and wanted to tell me about it. He sounded very sick and scared. I called him right back, but couldn't reach him. By the time I got to the house, he was unconscious."

"I want to help you find the killer, Latimer. You tell me what to do and I'll do it." He raised his head and looked at Latimer with determination. "This is it. I've had enough. I don't care which one of them did it, I will help you find him or her."

Latimer looked at him and tried to decide whether all this was an act or the real thing. He liked the man and hoped for the latter. However, he would not trust him to the point of confiding in him. The many years on the force had taught him better.

"Grant, I appreciate any effort you can make to help me. Keep your eyes and ears open to what is going on at your mother's house and among your siblings. Here's my card. Call me at any time, day or night, if you find something we can use." He got up and handed it to Grant. "I appreciate your honesty and hope the police and I can bring this case to a successful conclusion soon." He shook his hand. "I hope I can come and talk to you again should the need arise."

"Absolutely, I will call you should I find out anything of interest." He led Latimer to the door.

"By the way, the police will probably be here any minute to question you." Latimer saw a slight flicker in his eyes. He noticed Grant didn't ask him what hospital Henry had been taken to.

A gentle snow was falling as he drove back to the office.

Chapter 8

"They are a bunch of worthless, money hungry, spoiled people." Brighton made the announcement with disgust in his voice. He had called Latimer in the afternoon after interviewing the Hellman heirs. "The mother is the only decent one in the bunch. How in the world am I going to figure out which one of them did it, Latimer?" he added with frustration in his voice.

"What did you think of Grant Hellman?" Latimer asked.

"He was the nicest one of them all. Actually, quite a decent guy if I think about it. The worst of them is Allan. You just want to wring his scrawny, spoiled little neck."

Latimer laughed.

"Remember, don't let your emotions cloud your judgment. Facts are what counts. Trust me, I have made the mistake of letting my feelings for a suspect guide me many times. I still do at times."

"I know, but there is such a thing as disgusting. That guy fits the mold. I would like to haul him in and let him roast in a cell overnight. I bet he would give me a confession the next morning, whether he's guilty or not." Brighton was on a roll.

"I guess the case is solved then and we can all go home and rest easy." Latimer was still laughing. "Have you considered, if he didn't do it, he will come into fifty million dollars?"

"I wish someone would give me that kind of money." Brighton said with a deep sigh.

"I wonder if you would turn out just like him. You never know." Latimer said.

"You think I would, Latimer?" He sounded shocked.

"I don't think we need to worry about that any time soon. On the other hand, I can't imagine you ever turning out like that guy, no matter what happens, Kid."

"You haven't called me Kid in a long time. I sort of miss it."

"It slipped out. I was thinking this morning, what a good detective you've become with the way you took charge of the crime scene today. On the other hand, to me, you'll always be the Kid."

"Then I can ask you the question I always used to ask. 'Where do we go from here?'

Latimer chuckled.

"That does bring back the old days when we worked together, doesn't it?" He looked at Brighton with affection. "What did I always tell you when I didn't know?"

"Something is going to happen to open up the case." Brighton said without hesitation.

"That's it. The best thing is to sleep on it and start fresh in the morning. Why don't you and I both do that and go home before we get snowed in. Do me a favor and keep calling the hospital to check on Henry. If he wakes up, we need to go see him right away, before someone gets to him again."

Latimer looked out the window as the white, fluffy stuff continued to come down at a steady pace.

"You hang in there and I'll talk to you tomorrow," he said before he hung up.

With the weather being what it was, there was no choice but to call Glenda to cancel their dinner plans. The streets would be too dangerous.

"Sue Ellen, you better go home right now before it gets worse out there. If the streets aren't cleared, you stay home tomorrow. Make sure you turn the phones and the computer over to your apartment." He handed her his recorder. "Here's something for you to transcribe."

"Ok, Latimer darlin'."

He smiled. He was sure she was the best secretary he could have ever found.

Glenda was already home by the time he got there. Everyone in the office was allowed to leave because of the weather. She had taken out chicken and was busy in the kitchen.

"We're having southern fried chicken tonight. Sue Ellen gave me the recipe not too long ago and I'm going to try it. The girl swore it was the best thing since sliced bread."

"That's not really what she said, is it?" Latimer asked.

"No, I think she put it this way, 'It's better than Georgia ice cream on a cold morning' or something like that. I've wondered ever since what Georgia ice cream was."

Latimer laughed. "I asked her that one day. It's cheese grits. I'm getting an education at the University of Adell, Georgia."

Glenda laughed.

"How are you coming on your case, honey?" she asked.

"I talked to Brighton this afternoon. He is worried as usual that he won't solve the attempted murder of Henry Gossomer in one day."

"He's a sweet young man and I hope you'll help him." She patted the chicken dry.

"Of course I will. Right now I don't know any more than he does." Latimer was sitting on a stool in front of the kitchen counter and watched her prepare the meal.

"You have no idea which of the kids might be the one?" She looked at him.

"I don't. It's way too early. What I want to do is get them all together in one room and interview them at the same time. It would be great to see how they interact. I think I will try to do that next weekend."

"No, you won't. Next weekend is the big party for Cassie and Jerry."

"Oops, I forgot. We'll get to show off our fine threads to the world of corporate America. I call it snobsville." He chuckled.

"You're terrible. Remember, Cassie is one of them." Glenda looked at him with a frown. "Jerry's attitude is rubbing off on you, Mr. Latimer."

The phone rang.

"Saved by the bell," he said as he took out his cell phone.

"Latimer here."

It was Brighton.

"I called the hospital. Henry is still in a coma and they expect him to stay that way for the next few days."

"Are they sure he's going to survive?"

"I asked the nurse and she said it is touch and go. The next twenty-four hours will be critical. She did say, no one has come to see him so far, it may be because of the weather." He sounded sad. "You'd think the Hellman's would have someone come out to see how he is doing."

"Did she say any of them called?" Latimer asked.

"I think she would have mentioned that when I asked her," he said. "I guess you're not coming in tomorrow morning until the snow has been cleared?"

"No way, it's too dangerous," Latimer said "You stay safe going home, Kid."

The next morning Latimer looked out of the kitchen window. The street in front of the condo was covered in deep snow. This part of town was not on the VIP list of the city to be cleared, and it would probably be noon before they would get here. There was no newspaper either. He turned on the TV and found out, the entire city of Glenridge, and most of the State, was buried under six to ten inches of snow. He might as well relax and enjoy the day off with Glenda. He called Sue Ellen and told her to stay home until the roads were cleared.

"You already had a call this morning, darlin'. It was Grant Hellman. He says he has something to tell you. He'll call you on the cell phone shortly."

Latimer wondered what that was all about as he hung up. His phone rang almost immediately. It was Grant.

"Latimer, I'm sorry to bother you, but something occurred to me last night. I was at my mom's house, and so were Becky, Sylvia and Allan. We were talking about Dad. After a while the conversation heated up and we all started yelling at each other. Except for Becky, she just sat there and smiled. When we finally stopped, she told us that we should be glad someone had the guts to make it possible for us to finally get the money we deserved."

"Did she say she killed him?" Latimer asked.

"No, she didn't, but she might as well have. We all looked at each other, wondering the same thing. I finally asked her right out. She smiled at me and said, 'It's for me to know and for you to find out'. My mom got really upset and told her not to talk such nonsense. Becky yelled back at her that everyone, including Mom, was glad he was dead. It was terrible, Latimer. What a family!" He sounded angry. "When I asked her if she tried to kill Henry as well, she just laughed and said, he was only a servant and who cared."

"Thank you for telling me about this. Did you notice anyone else reacting in an unusual way to her remarks?

"Just my mom. She told all of us, she was absolutely sure none of us was a murderer and to stop talking such nonsense. I really didn't look at the others. I was too busy wondering about Becky."

"Keep up the good work, Grant. It saves me from interviewing everyone again," Latimer said. "I'll talk to you later."

"Are you going to tell Becky I told you about her?"

"I don't think so, if you are to continue to report to me what goes on in your family."

Latimer was deep in thought when he hung up. Could he trust this guy or was he just playing him to throw him off track? It was simply too early to tell. He reached for the phone and called Brighton.

"Can you have someone check the database and see if any of the Hellman kids have a record?"

"Do you have something on any of them?" Brighton asked. "I could sure use a break."

Latimer told him about his conversation with Grant.

"I don't know if I can trust the guy yet. Don't put too much into this. Let's see first what the database tells us. Call me when you're done. I'm at home. I'm surprised you made it to work."

"I have a four-wheel drive. A little bit of snow doesn't bother me."

He could almost see Brighton grin over the phone.

The rest of the morning went quiet. Glenda spent the whole time on the phone with her work. A lot of it had to do with getting everything arranged with the staff of the Granger Hotel for the preparation of the company event. He admired how professional she sounded and decided, she was made for that job.

The snow removal crew came after lunch. By two o'clock, Latimer was on his way to the precinct. He wanted to see if Brighton had found anything. Before he got to his office, he ran into Inspector Harold Brown. All he got from him was an icy stare. He wondered if there ever would be a chance for them to get back on speaking terms again. Apparently, today was not the day. They had been in a good-natured competition of who would solve the most cases before retirement. However, when Latimer solved a case a few weeks ago that Brown had failed to crack, the casual rivalry turned into open hostility on Brown's side.

Brighton was not in his office and Latimer walked over to the database room. He saw him hunched over in front of the screen as the information whizzed by with lightening speed. He looked up when Latimer stood next to him.

"So far I've found nothing. I'm checking on Grant Hellman now. Suddenly the screen stopped at the picture of Grant W. Hellman. "Well, what do you know? The boy has a record."

Latimer leaned closer to read what it said.

"It's for reckless vehicular endangerment, drunk driving, and several misdemeanors for disturbing the peace under the influence at the country club. It's your typical spoiled, rich kid antics, nothing serious. The old man paid the fines and he was let go with several stints of community service." Brighton was disappointed. "Nothing we can get him on with this case."

"Now I can understand why the father mentioned him being wild on the video. Let's try Allan W. Hellman," Latimer said.

It turned out, he didn't have a record and neither did the other siblings.

"I think I'll have a talk with Rebecca Hellman again," Latimer said. "On second thought, why don't you make an appointment to see her and I'll go with you. This way she can't turn us down. We need to ask her about those comments she made and pose a few more questions about her attitude with her father, the butler and the inheritance."

"Let's call her right now." Brighton dialed her number when they got back to his office. He told her they would be there in thirty minutes to talk to her.

They drove up in the police car and were allowed into the condo by the doorman, without fuss when Brighton showed his badge. The same young maid opened the door and led them into the living room. Becky was looking out of the window with a glass of wine in her hand.

"I didn't know you were still with the police, Mr. Latimer," she said in a friendly tone.

"I'm not, Ma'am. I'm working with them at the moment to solve the attempt on Henry Gossomer's life. Since both, your father's case and his, are connected, I thought it would be easier if I came with Det. Sgt. Brighton to ask you some more questions." Latimer spoke in his most easygoing voice.

"Ask away, gentlemen. I'm in a good mood at the moment." She took another sip of wine. Latimer saw she was drunk.

Brighton nodded to him to continue.

"I have a question about the rather unusual comments you made yesterday afternoon to your family. How did you say it, when your brother Grant asked you if you killed your father? 'It is for me to know and for you to find out'? Can you tell us what you meant by that exactly, Ma'am?"

She looked at both of them with an astonished expression. Her lips formed a tiny pout and her eyes had a hard time focusing.

"I didn't mean anything by that. I said it to make Grant mad. He sounded so high and mighty. Who knows, maybe he is the one who killed Father. I certainly did not." She spoke with exaggerated emphasis and slurred her words slightly.

"In these circumstances, Ms. Hellman, it is rather foolish to make such statements. You must remember, we don't know when you want to get your brother mad or when you are confessing to the murder of your father. Let's not forget, trying to poison the butler." Brighton looked at her with a severe look on his face. "On the basis of that statement, I could bring you in for questioning. I will need a better explanation than that."

She was stunned at first. Then her face changed from casual friendliness to sadness and then to crying. She suddenly looked like a little girl as the tears rolled down her beautiful face.

"I didn't mean anything by it. You can't talk to me that way. I didn't kill my father, honest. I just wanted them to stop fighting. I hate it when they fight. It upsets me terribly, just like you're upsetting me right now." She reached for a tissue with a dramatic gesture and delicately wiped the few tears she had managed to squeeze out.

Latimer and Brighton sat and watched in silence.

"That was a great performance, Ms. Hellman, but not quite great enough," Brighton finally said with perfect calm. He smiled at her. "I don't fool that easy, not even with a beautiful woman like you. Why don't you tell us the truth instead, and confess you killed your father and tried the same with Henry." His tone had taken on a hardness Latimer had rarely heard before.

"You stupid little policeman!" She jumped up and screamed at him. "Who do you think I am? Some little tramp you can harass and impress with your badge? Remember, I will be inheriting more money than you'll ever see in your lifetime." She still held the glass in her hand. As she pointed it at Brighton, most of the wine spilled on the floor.

When she realized what had happened, she threw the glass at him. He ducked and it missed.

"That does it, Ms. Hellman. You are under arrest for assaulting a police officer." With a few practiced motions, he handcuffed her and then read her her Miranda rights. She kept screaming obscenities at him throughout. He never lost his calm.

Latimer stood by and didn't interfere. The Kid handled it just fine.

The maid stood and watched, terrified.

"Call my lawyer, Rachel," Becky screamed on the way out. "He will sue you blind and you'll never work again, you miserable little man." She tried to spit at Brighton, but missed.

He forced her into the elevator and then into the car without saying a word.

"That went well, Sir." He grinned as Latimer got into the passenger seat. They both laughed. It reminded them of the times they had worked together in similar difficult situations in the past. Both ignored Becky's continued ranting in the backseat.

Latimer didn't go in with Brighton.

"Let me know if you find out anything useful before her lawyer gets here," he said as he opened the door to his car. It was time to go home before it got dark. It looked like more snow was on the way. He stopped by the deli and ordered dinner for two.

Chapter 9

The next morning brought a clear, blue sky with temperatures in the twenty's. The roads were made treacherous with ice pockets when Latimer drove to the office. Brighton called him before he got there.

"I'm going to the hospital this morning to see Henry. Do you want to come along, Latimer?" He sounded cheerful as usual. "The nurse called me. Henry woke up."

Latimer turned the car around and headed for the hospital. He got there fifteen minutes later. Brighton's car was already there. The nurse showed them to Henry's room.

"He is very weak. I don't know if he can talk, but you can try," she said. "Make sure you don't upset him or tire him out too much."

The curtains were closed and the room was dimly lit. Henry Gossomer lay still, with several tubes hooked up to both arms. His eyes were closed.

"Henry, it's Latimer, can you hear me?"

The butler opened his eyes slowly and looked at Latimer and Brighton without recognition at first.

"I'm the detective you called before you got sick, remember?" Latimer spoke softly. "We're here to ask you if you know who poisoned you."

There was no reaction. Henry continued to look at him, trying to focus his eyes.

"Henry, this is important. You told me you found something in Mr. Hellman's bedroom. Can you remember what it was?" Latimer leaned over him.

Henry tried to speak. He moved his eyes in Latimer's direction. His lips moved slightly and a faint sound came out of his mouth. Latimer leaned closer over his mouth, trying to hear.

"Camera… tape in room. My bed..look."

That's all Latimer could understand.

"What kind of camera, Henry, and what room? Mr. Hellman's room?"

Henry nodded his head in the affirmative with a barely noticeable move.

"There is a camera in Mr. Hellman's room? Is that it, Henry?"

Another nod, weaker this time.

"Is the tape in Mr. Hellman's room?"

Henry shook his head in the negative.

"Henry, just blink your eyes once for 'yes' and twice for 'no'," Latimer said.

"There is a camera in Mr. Hellman's room and you found it?"

He blinked once.

"The tape is in the same room?"

He blinked twice.

"The tape is in your room?"

Henry blinked once.

"Is it a video camera?"

He blinked twice.

"Is it a camera installed in the room somewhere?"

He blinked once.

"Is it in the ceiling?"

Henry's eyes closed. He was unconscious again.

"Brighton, I guess, Henry found a secret camera in Mr. Hellman's room. I bet he had it installed without anyone knowing about it." Latimer sounded excited. "What I think happened, the murderer found the camera, but not the tape. Henry did and hid the tape in his room and called me to give it to me. From what he tried to tell me, it is still hidden in his room."

"We need to get a search warrant for Henry's room," Brighton said. "I'll call the Chief." He took out his cell phone and told Chief Carson what happened. His face fell when he hung up. The Chief doesn't think there is enough evidence to convince a judge."

"You may need a warrant, Brighton, but I don't. We'll go over to the Hellman's estate and I will simply ask if I can take a look at Henry's room. I'm pretty sure Patricia Hellman will allow me to do that."

He looked at Henry Gossomer. The man was sleeping or in a coma, he didn't know. On the way out they ran into Grant Hellman.

"How is Henry?" He asked Latimer. "I came to see him." He seemed genuinely concerned.

"He recognized me when I talked to him," Latimer said. "I'm afraid he's asleep again. We didn't talk to the doctor to ask how he's doing."

"Come with me to the nurse's station and I'll see if we can ask someone," Grant said.

There was no doctor available and the nurse in charge told them she could not give them that information, since they were not family.

"Can you at least tell me if he's going to make it?" Grant sounded impatient.

"I'm sorry, I can't."

"Nurse, he doesn't have any family. He is our butler, we are his family."

"What is your name, Sir?" she asked and looked at the chart in her hand.

"Grant Hellman."

"I see here that Mrs. Patricia Hellman is listed as a person to be notified in case of an emergency." The nurse looked at Grant, uncertain what to do.

"I'm her son." He turned to Brighton. "Det. Sgt. Brighton can verify that fact."

"I sure can, Ma'am. I'm with the Glenridge Major Crime Unit and I believe you can tell us about the status of Mr. Gossomer. He is part of an ongoing investigation."

"In that case, I suppose its ok." She turned to Grant. "Mr. Gossomer is in stable, but critical condition. Not knowing what the poison is, we cannot give him an antidote. He could take a turn for the worse at any time if his body is not strong enough to fight the poison on his own. His heart has suffered and the doctor is giving him heart medication to stabilize it. It is still touch and go. We should know more by tomorrow. It takes that long for the poison to lose its potency." She closed the chart and smiled. "That is all I can tell you, Mr. Hellman."

"Thank you, nurse. I really appreciate it." Grant sounded relieved. "Did he say anything to you when he was awake?" he asked Latimer as they walked to the elevator.

"Didn't you forget to stop by his room, Grant?" Latimer said.

"Oh, my goodness, I did. I guess I'm too upset to think clearly right now." He slapped his forehead. "I'll go back right now. I'll see you later." He turned around and walked back to the room.

Latimer stopped Brighton from entering the elevator.

"I'm going to follow him and listen at the door to see what he does. You wait here for me." Latimer walked slowly back to the room to give Grant time to go in. He stood outside the door and stuck his head around the door opening. He saw Grant standing by the bedside, holding Henry's hand. Latimer couldn't see his face.

"You're in a lot of trouble, Henry. I'm sorry. I wish you could tell me how much you know." Latimer could hear the worlds clearly.

Without hesitation he walked into the room.

"I'm sorry, but I think I forgot my cell phone in here. Have you seen it, Grant?" Latimer pretended to look around.

"I haven't seen anything, Latimer." His voice sounded gruff.

"Sorry to intrude," Latimer said and left.

"Brighton, you need to tell the nurse not to let anyone come into the room by themselves. I have a feeling, whoever tried to kill him, will try again." Latimer told Brighton what he overheard. They went back to the nurse's station.

"Nurse, can you see to it that no visitors are allowed in unless someone is with them until Mr. Gossomer wakes up tomorrow? There has been an attempt on his life and we believe the person will try again," Brighton told her.

"Does that go for family members?" She asked.

"Especially the family members, Ma'am," he said.

"I don't understand. You just had me tell Grant Hellman about his condition. He's a family member." She was confused.

"Something has come up, Ma'am and the situation has changed," Brighton said and gave her one of his bright smiles. "As a matter of fact, please have someone go into the room right now. Grant Hellman is still in there by himself."

The nurse walked to the room immediately and escorted Grant out. Latimer and Brighton hid around the corner and waited until he got on the elevator.

"It could've been a very innocent remark, Brighton," Latimer said. "He is a nice guy and the only one who has come to visit. He could also be the murderer, and that's why he came to see Henry. We can't take the chance."

"Are we coming back tomorrow to see Henry?" Brighton asked.

Latimer laughed. "You're forgetting you're in charge again, Kid."

"I guess I am." Brighton looked at Latimer with a sheepish grin. "It happens every time I'm around you."

"I have a feeling, if the murderer didn't find the tape in Henry's room, he or she will try again. I wish we could move him somewhere safe." Latimer sounded concerned. "It won't matter if he is still in the hospital or at the Hellman estate. The man is in definite danger."

Latimer reached in his pocket and pulled out his cell phone.

"I'm going to call Patricia Hellman and ask her if we can come by this afternoon and check out Henry's room.

They were on their way to the estate when Latimer's phone rang.

"Can we have that dinner date tonight, the one we missed last week because of the snow?" Glenda sounded cheerful. "I don't feel like cooking. "I can meet you at your office at six."

"I'm on my way to the Hellman's right now. I should be done by then. Meet me at the precinct, because I'm with Brighton. We can go to the Garden House. That way you get a salad and I can get a steak."

"That sounds wonderful. See you then, handsome."

"I'm glad you two are happy, Latimer. I knew, when I met her the first time, she was for you, didn't I?" Brighton smiled. She is the nicest lady you could've ever found."

"I agree with you. Now we need to work on you getting hitched. How is Hattie Mansfield these days?" You haven't said anything lately."

"We are getting along just fine. The wedding will definitely be in June. She has a huge family, so it won't be a small affair. Her parents are very nice people and I go there for dinner a lot. My folks like her, too. They think she's perfect for me." He sounded happy.

"There is nothing better than a good marriage, but there is nothing worse than a bad one, my mother used to say. She was a wise woman," Latimer said. "I've been fortunate twice in my life. I can't ask for more. I can only hope you will be as happy as I've been with the two women I married, son."

"I have a feeling we'll do ok, Latimer. Hattie is not only pretty, she's nice as well." Brighton had a dreamy look on his face. "It feels great to be in love."

The gate was open when they arrived at the Hellman estate and drove up to the house on the snow-packed driveway. The grounds looked like a fairy tale land with white caps on every branch. Smoke curled up from a chimney in the main house.

A maid greeted them as they arrived at the front door.

"Please, come in, Mrs. Hellman is waiting for you," she said and led them to the family room. The view out of the large windows overlooking the white, rolling landscape was like a wonderland. Patricia got up from her chair as they walked in.

"It is good to see you. Please, have a seat. I want to hear how Henry is doing. I hear from Grant that you went to see him today."

"He is still in critical condition and will be so for the next few days, Mrs. Hellman," Brighton said. "Until the poison is gone from his body, his heart can still give out."

"Oh my goodness, the poor man, I would have gone to see him, but the weather has been simply too dreadful." She sat back down in her chair.

"We would like to go over his room one more time, if that is ok with you, Ma'am," Latimer said. "We may have missed something," Latimer said in a casual tone.

"It has been thoroughly cleaned by the staff. I can't see what it is you're looking for. Whatever evidence there was, it is gone by now." She suddenly looked tense.

"I realize it is an imposition, Mrs. Hellman, but since I've been hired by your late husband to look into his murder, it is imperative that I have access to all matters related to his death." Latimer sounded firm.

"Are you saying that this incident with Henry is related to William's death?"

"That is what I'm saying. They are pretty sure the same poison was used with both men, and that makes it part of the case." Latimer looked at her with a stern expression. He noticed the reluctance, before she finally agreed.

"I guess there is nothing I can do but go along with this. I'm not pleased about it, Mr. Latimer." There was a touch of anger in her voice.

Latimer chose to ignore it.

"We will be quite a while and will let you know when we're done," he said in a casual manner. You may have to have the staff straighten it out after we're done. We may even look into Mr. Hellman's bedroom before we're done. It depends on what we find."

Patricia Hellman stared out the window, ignoring his remarks.

On the way up the stairs, Brighton whispered to Latimer, "That went well." He was smiling.

They stood in the doorway to Henry's room. It was clean and orderly.

"There is no need to look in the obvious places like drawers or the likes. Why don't you check every pocket of every piece of clothing in the closet, Brighton? I'll look in the room and bathroom. Make sure you knock against the back wall of the closet. There may be a secret space behind it. He's lived here a long time, there's bound to be a special hiding place somewhere." Latimer stood and looked around the room for a long time without moving.

For two hours they checked every inch of the room, the walls, every possible place and even the impossible ones. Brighton ended up with soot on his face when he reached up into the fireplace, but found nothing.

"We're not giving up," Latimer said as he blew his nose because of the dust they had stirred up. He stood, looking and thinking what they might have missed. Finally, he walked over to the corner of the room on the right side of the bed and reached down to pull up the rug, but found nothing. He continued with the other side. When he got to the fourth corner, he felt something underneath the rug. When he pulled it up, it was a small tape from a surveillance camera.

"Bingo! Here it is, Kid." He held it up triumphantly. "Thank you, Henry!" He kissed it. "We've struck gold."

"I will take that," a voice said from behind. It was Allan. "This is our property and you have no right to take it, Mr. Latimer." His voice sounded menacing. "Give it to me."

"I don't think so, Mr. Hellman," Brighton said. "We will hand it over to your lawyer until we can get a court order."

"You have no right to do that and I won't let you." He looked angry and filled the door with a defiant stance.

"In that case we will simply stay here until someone from the precinct brings the search warrant." Brighton reached for his cell phone and called the Chief and explained the situation to him. "It will be here in thirty minutes, Sir. Until then, we'll just make ourselves comfortable right here in this room."

"I'm going to have to ask you to leave right this moment." It was Patricia Hellman. "But not before you give me the tape." She reached out her hand as she walked into the room.

"I'm sorry, Ma'am, that's not going to happen. I will arrest you, just like I did your daughter, if you give me any trouble." He stood his ground and stared at her with an authoritative look. "This is evidence, and it will remain in our possession until the search warrant gets here."

"You have no right to do this," Allan was shouting by now. "This is private property. Do you have any idea who you're messing with?" His face was red and he took a threatening stance toward Latimer.

"According to your father's Will, I have every right. Give me enough reason and I will see to it that the fifty million dollars you want so badly, will be given to charity. Then again, it may happen anyway since you certainly sound like you're the one who poisoned him, or you wouldn't be so eager to get your hands on the tape." Latimer stared him down and Allan backed off.

"Mom, do something," he said in a whiny tone as he turned to his mother. "You're not going to let him talk to me that way, are you Mom?"

"It's alright, baby. I'm calling the lawyer. He'll straighten this whole mess out." She turned around and walked downstairs, followed by Allan.

"That went well," Brighton said with a big grin. "This is some awful family. It makes me glad I don't have any money. No one would ever treat me the way these people treated Mr. Hellman. No wonder he made a Will like he did." He sat in the chair with the tape in his hand. "I wonder which one of them did it."

"There is no doubt in my mind one of these two did it," Latimer said. Maybe both of them, the way they're acting."

"That reminds me," Brighton said, "Becky Hellman was bailed out by the lawyer. She was much calmer after a night in jail. I think she'll think twice before spitting at me again." He was laughing. "It always amazes me what a calming effect a jail cell has on most people."

Within the hour, both the lawyer and the search warrant came. Mrs. Hellman and Allan were told by Gary Norton there was nothing he could do. He came upstairs to talk to Latimer and Brighton.

"I see you found something interesting," he said with a straight face, careful not to let them know how he really felt. After all, the Hellman's were his clients.

"You will be glad to know, Henry is still alive, Mr. Norton," Latimer said. "We went to see him this morning. He's the one who told us to look in his room for a tape. There must be a hidden camera in Mr.

Hellman's bedroom. That's how he knew someone poisoned him. Why he wouldn't tell you who it was, I don't know. I'm sure it will be revealed when take a good look at it."

"That means the case will be solved any time now?" Gary Norton sounded amazed.

"Not until we see what's on the tape. There maybe nothing on there we can use," Brighton said. "I'll take it to our lab and let the boys see what they can come up with." He put the tape into a plastic bag.

Brighton and Latimer were on their way back to the precinct. It would be tomorrow before they would find out anything, because it was near quitting time. Latimer had just enough time to get back and wait for Glenda. He was happy. At least they had a fresh lead and the two of them could discuss the case. It was another benefit of being married to this wonderful woman. They spent a lot of evenings sharing what happened during the day. She was a great help to him to be able to think out loud about a case, and bounce different theories and possibilities off of her. He wondered if she didn't rather prefer to talk tonight about the upcoming event at the Granger Hotel. He felt sorry for Jerry. The boy must be petrified by the prospect to be paraded in front of the VIPs of a large corporation.

Chapter 10

It was early the next morning. Latimer was on his way to the precinct. Brighton had called and asked him to accompany him to the hospital. He thought Henry would talk more if Latimer asked the questions, since he knew him.

When they arrived at Henry's room, the bed was freshly made and empty. They went to the nurse's station. Brighton flashed his badge and asked for the whereabouts of Henry Gossomer.

"Mr. Gossomer died last night, Officer," the nurse said. "He never regained consciousness since you saw him yesterday." It was the same nurse.

"Did he have any visitors since we saw him?" Latimer asked.

"Yes, there were several family members who came to see him. I cannot tell you who they were since I was no longer on duty. The next shift didn't take down names of course. The instructions read that no one could go in alone. The LPN made sure of that, but she did not stay with them."

"Could we talk to her, please?" Latimer asked.

"She will be back on duty tonight. If you would like to come back then, I'm sure she'll be glad to talk to you."

"Is there to be an autopsy?" Brighton asked.

"I have no idea, but I did hear the coroner's people came to pick up the body last night. So I imagine there will be. If there is nothing else, I have to go."

"Thank you, nurse."

"I wonder if someone got to him, or if he died of the first round of poison," Brighton said to Latimer.

"It doesn't really matter in the end, does it? Whoever gave him the first dose, will be charged with murder. There is no law that says you can murder someone twice." Latimer said with a grin. "They may have been there just to visit. It was about time. After all, Henry had worked for them for twenty years. That should count for something.

"I will have to come back tonight and ask the LPN if she remembers who was there to visit the man last night." Brighton sighed. "I have a date with Hattie. Maybe I can bring her with me, and afterwards we can still make the movies."

"Wow, some date. Are you sure she will go along with that?" Latimer asked.

"I know she will. She thinks I walk on water since I learned from you. She wants to learn my techniques so she can work in the Major Crime Unit a few years down the road." Brighton was a little embarrassed. "I told her I wasn't near as good as you, but she thinks I am."

"Don't disappoint her then. You are a good detective."

They drove into the precinct parking lot.

"Let me know what you find out. I'm going back to the office. I'll see you later." Latimer said as he got out of the car.

Sue Ellen was sitting at her desk typing,

"Good mornin' Latimer, darlin'. You have three messages. One is from that swanky lawyer Gary Norton. He wants to talk to you when you have a minute. The other is from Mrs. Hellman. She sounded winy and upset as usual. The last is from that lovely wife of yours. She wants you to remind you of their dinner date tonight." She handed him the slips with the messages.

Latimer dialed Gary Norton and sat down at his desk.

"I would like to talk to you about the tape," Gary Norton said. "Have you looked at it yet?" He asked Latimer. Mrs. Hellman is terribly upset and wants it back. I told her it was obtained legally and there was nothing I could do. Because of client confidentiality, all I can do is that you ask her about Becky."

"What about Becky?" Latimer was confused.

"I can't say any more than that. Just ask her. She said she would call you." He sounded tense.

"She did call and left a message with my secretary. I will call her back when I hang up with you. What should I say?"

"Just say you need to know about Becky."

"That's it?" Latimer asked.

"Yes. I've said too much already. Have a nice day, Mr. Latimer."

That was definitely strange. He dialed Patricia's number.

"Mr. Latimer, how good of you to call back." She sounded polite and friendly. Not at all like yesterday.

"Mrs. Hellman, what can I do for you?" He asked.

"I need to talk to you about one of my children. Can you come by the house this morning?"

"Does this have to do with your husband's death or Henry's?"

"Henry died? I had no idea, no one notified me. I know my name was on the list in case of an emergency. Why didn't anyone call me?"

"I will be there in half an hour, Mrs. Hellman and we can talk about this," he said.

"I will be waiting for you, Mr. Latimer." She hung up.

Latimer stopped by Sue Ellen's desk on his way out.

"I'll be at the Hellman estate. You can call me on my cell phone if there is anything important."

"I need to get off on time this afternoon. I have a date," she said before he left. "Should I switch the phone over to your cell when I leave?"

"That sounds good. Have fun." He put his heavy coat on. It was still very cold outside. The air was crisp and clear with a faint whiff of burning wood. The snow was still on the ground, except for the streets and driveways. He loved this kind of dry cold.

When he arrived at the Hellman estate, the maid opened the front door. It looked like she had taken over the job from Henry. Brighton had been there most of the morning. The case had gone from attempted murder to murder. He wondered if that's what Patricia wanted to talk to him about.

"Please follow me to the family room, Sir," she said.

Patricia Hellman was sitting on the couch facing the beautiful white scenery outside the large windows. She got up when he entered the room and held out her hand with a charming smile. He wondered what she wanted, given her sudden friendly attitude.

"Come on in, Mr. Latimer. I appreciate you coming to talk to me. This is a sad house without Henry. We're all going to miss him terribly." She dabbed her face with a tissue. Her dramatics reminded him of Becky before she went ballistic on him the other day.

"What is it I can do for you, Mrs. Hellmann?" He was curious.

"My husband hired you to investigate his murder. With what's happened to Henry, it really looks like he was right. I'm worried about my children. I love them and would not wish any one of them to go to prison. I absolutely can't imagine any of them doing this terrible thing, but I have to admit, it certainly looks like one of them did."

"Do you have a suspicion?" He was intrigued by her line of thought.

"I don't have any idea, but at the same time, Allan is behaving very odd lately. I can't put my finger on it. He keeps asking me for money and no matter how much I give him, it's gone. When I ask him what he does with it, he gives me an evasive answer. I think he's on drugs, Mr. Latimer. I can see it in his eyes sometimes. They look glassy and his speech is slurred."

"If that is true, it would definitely be a motive for murder," Latimer said. "How about Becky, what can you tell me about her?" He held his breath.

"Funny you should ask me about her. She is acting even stranger. She and Allan are really close these days. They used to hate each other, but now they have secret meetings to which I'm not invited. Since she was arrested, she is in constant contact with Allan. He's over at her place right now."

"Are you saying the two are conspiring to cover up the murder of your husband and Henry?" He was wondering for a second why a doting mother would want to accuse two of the children.

"I would never go so far as to say that, Mr. Latimer, but it does look like they're getting together about something I don't know about." She looked at him with a sad expression. "It is terrible for me to say those things, but I don't know what else to do."

"Have you spoken to Becky or Allan about this?" Latimer asked.

"No, I don't dare. They both have a violent temper and if they are guilty, they might do something to me." She was crying by now.

"Why would those two kill your husband, Mrs. Hellman?"

"I think I've spoiled them too much and they couldn't wait for their inheritance."

"How about Sylvia, Grant and William, don't you think they were also impatient? Especially Sylvia, she doesn't have any income like the others and only gets a paltry sum each month," he asked.

"You have a point. Let's face it, they all hated William. I feel sorry for them. He did make it difficult to live on the small amount he gave them." Her voice was filled with pity.

"Are you telling me, you think they were mistreated by you husband, because he didn't give them everything they wanted?" Latimer tried hard to hide his astonishment.

"All I know, William and I used to fight about it all the time. Even in death he has cheated them. What if you can't solve this case, they'll get nothing for ten years. That is so very cruel. You have no idea how my children have counted on their inheritance. As their mother, I want to help you solve this case as soon as possible." She looked at him as if to ask for approval.

"Let me put this into perspective. You are telling me, that two of your children might be involved in the two murders. You want to help me catch them so the others can claim their inheritance?" He tried very hard to sound casual.

"That's right. I have the money to hire the best lawyers in the country. If they did do it, I'll get them off for some reason or another." She leaned over towards him. "Don't you see, if I point you in the right direction, you will solve the case and then everyone gets their money. Whoever doesn't, I'll help them when they are done with the trial and all that."

He looked at her with an expression of utter amazement. He wondered if she was mentally ill. Maybe she really believed, whichever one of her children killed two people, would get off, because she could afford a good lawyer. No wonder Gary Norton wanted him to go see her. He was sure the man had told her it wouldn't work, but apparently she did not want to listen to him.

"Mrs. Hellman, I can't agree with your logic. No one gets off after killing two people, no matter how good their lawyer is."

She looked at him with a look of pity.

"Mr. Latimer, in your position in life you have no idea what money can do. After all, a policeman doesn't make enough to understand our kind of people. I feel sorry for those who don't have as much as we do, but I suppose you can't miss what you've never had. I've been told, most poor people enjoy being poor." She leaned back with a satisfied smile. "What would they do if they didn't have us to give them a job to make a decent living? My children have always had everything and wouldn't know how to get along without a lot of income."

It was all Latimer could do not to walk out on her. He had to wait to calm down before he could find his voice.

"I'm sure you're right, Mrs. Hellman," he finally managed to say.

"I'm glad we understand each other, Mr. Latimer. I hope I've helped you today with your case and we can come to a conclusion soon so that my children can enjoy life again after all this dreary business." She got up and held out her hand. "Thank you for being so understanding. Jessica will see you out."

Latimer had to sit in his car for quite a while before he was able to drive. He was shaking with anger. How could a nice man like William Hellman have ever put up with a horrible family like that? He had dealt with a lot of despicable criminals in his thirty years, but never with a group this selfish, arrogant and heartless. When he finally started the car, his hands were still shaking. He drove to the precinct to see if they had found anything on the tape from Henry's room.

Brighton was in his office going over the preliminary coroner's report for Henry. It looked like his heart gave out from the effects of the poison. There was nothing else wrong with him. In other words, the butler could have lived for many more years.

"I'm sorry this man had to die because of that despicable family," Latimer said in a harsh tone. "None of them deserved a faithful servant like Henry." He sat down and told Brighton what Patricia Hellman had said to him.

"I'm glad I wasn't there. I would've given the old bat a piece of my mind," Brighton said. "I sure misjudged her by thinking she was a nice lady."

"That's the first time in my career I almost lost my temper with people involved with a case," Latimer said. "I still don't understand why she wanted me to know Allan might be on drugs and in cahoots with Becky. Something's not right there. Personally, I think the woman doesn't have all her marbles together." He got up. "I need a cup of coffee. Can I get you one, Brighton?"

"That would be great. We can go to the lab and see what the boys have gotten off that tape. While you get the coffee I'll call them and see if we can take a look."

They walked to the lab, coffee in hand.

"I can't wait to see if we can make out anything interesting on that tape," Brighton said. "This is what Henry was killed for."

The lab technician was ready for them when they got there.

"There is a lot of activity on this tape. I have no idea if anything on there will help you with your case. Here it is," he pointed to a computer screen and left Latimer and Brighton to watch.

The picture was in black and white and quite grainy. They could make out Patricia Hellman come in and sit in the chair next to the bed. William Hellman looked very sick. This tape was definitely made after the taping of the Will, because he looked much worse. Jessica, the maid, could be seen several times bringing him something to eat. Allan stood there without saying a word each time he came in. Mr. Hellman was saying something to him, but since there was no sound, they could not guess what it was.

Grant came in several times. He talked to his father and actually leaned over and kissed him on the forehead before he left. Becky walked in with a glass of wine in her hand and they could see she was drunk. William, the oldest did not show up at all. Sylvia came once and stood in a detached posture, without saying anything as far as they could tell.

"What is wrong with the sound?" Latimer asked Brighton.

"They told me it didn't have any."

"You mean it was erased?" Latimer asked.

"No sound was recorded. I guess Mr. Hellman just wanted a record of who came to see him," Brighton said.

They continued to watch. Nothing much happened. Henry came in several times. They could see he asked Mr. Hellman if he needed anything. He refreshed the water pitcher and fluffed his pillows. Patricia never touched her husband in any way or tried to make him more comfortable. They were getting ready to give up when a dark figure walked into the room. It was impossible to tell who it was, or whether it was a man or a woman. It could have been in the evening or at night. The person was dressed in a bulky black parker. They must have known about the camera, because they never turned their head. Both Latimer and Brighton strained to see the item the person held in their hand. It looked like a needle. As they watched, the tape showed it being emptied into the IV going into Mr. Hellman's arm. They stood and watched in horror as the man gasped for a short while and then lay still. Right after, the murderer left the room.

"Holy Moses," Brighton said. "That was terrible. I couldn't make out a face, could you, Latimer?"

"No. They made sure not to turn toward the camera." Latimer inhaled deeply. "That was terrible." He turned to the technician at the next computer console. "Is there any way you guys can get us a face from this last scene?"

"We're working on it, but it will take time. We don't know yet if it's possible. We need to send it to a special lab in New York to reconstruct the face, taking the outline of the hood and what few details there are to work with. It can be several days before we hear anything. We made a copy of the tape and have sent it off this morning," he added.

"Thanks, Robert. Let me know when you get the report," Brighton said. "That's all we can get right now, I'm afraid," he said to Latimer on the way back to his office. "It would be nice if it showed us who the murderer is."

"At least we know it was one person, not two, according to the tape. On the other hand, they could have given him several doses over the last few weeks." Latimer said. "I'm on my way to the parking lot to meet Glenda. It's Friday and we're going out to dinner. I will see you next week. Give my regards to your lovely Hattie," he said as he walked to the elevator.

Tomorrow was the big shindig at the Granger Hotel.

Chapter 11

Anscott Research Laboratories had booked the entire Granger Hotel for Saturday. The entrance, the foyer and one of the ballrooms were decorated in a wedding motif. The second ballroom served as a dining room. A special Chef from New York was engaged to feed the five hundred guests for the fabulous dinner.

When Glenda told Latimer about the preparations, he cringed at the thought of Jerry having to face his "coming out party". Richard and Emily, together with Glenda and Latimer would be seated together at one of the front tables. Mr. and Mrs. Sanders, Jerry's parents, as well as his brother Michael and his sister Kathy and their spouses, would sit at one side of the happy couple at the head table. Mark Lenhart as CEO and Paul Carter, the Chairman of the Board and their spouses, would occupy the other side.

The table decorations for both ballrooms had been done by a large firm from New York. They were a stunning picture of elegance and beauty, with orchids and exotic greenery arranged artistically. There was almost as much silverware on the table as Jerry had predicted. He had practiced table etiquette diligently with Richard, as well as dealing with the important guests in attendance.

The festivities would begin at five with a cocktail party and hors devours. Cassie, Jerry and his family were scheduled to arrive at four-thirty. There would be a receiving line for the newlyweds, starting promptly at five. Glenda had talked with Jerry's family several days ago. She had informed them of the details of how everything was scheduled to work. They were not only excited, but understandably apprehensive about the whole thing. She tried to calm their fears and told them they would be just fine.

"Remember, your son is the guest of honor. Everyone will be extremely aware of that and treat you, his family, with the utmost politeness and respect. Just be yourselves and smile a lot as you are introduced. No one expects you to remember all their names." She tried to reassure them. "You are there to support Jerry. He has enough to deal with, without worrying about you."

Jerry's family arrived at two o'clock at the Estate and would be taken by limousine to the hotel. Cassie had asked them to come early. A fashion consultant was at hand to advise them on their outfits, hairstyle and make-up, if they needed improvements. The ladies were excited and didn't mind at all. Jerry's father and brother sat in the drawing room with Jerry and talked about the upcoming event. All three wore dark, formal suits with an orchid in their lapel. Richard had helped fasten them properly. The suits for Jerry's dad, his brother Michael and his sister Kathy's husband Frank, had been delivered two days ago by an expensive men's store in Glenridge. They all felt uncomfortable and unsure in their finery.

Latimer and Glenda joined them shortly thereafter.

"I hope this is not going to be as horrible as I imagine," Jerry said. "This suit alone is driving me crazy." He looked at his family with a sheepish grin. "If I survive this I can handle anything."

"You will survive this, son," his dad said with a firm voice. "You will do us proud. The only difference between you and them is, you are married to the boss and they're not." They laughed and everyone visibly relaxed.

"I never thought about that, Dad. Thanks. That helps me more than you can know." Jerry loved his dad. He was a man with a lot of commons sense, who had put today's event into perspective for him with one sentence.

At the last minute, Cassie decided, Jerry's parents should be part of the receiving line. She came to tell Jerry's dad.

"I want you and Claire to be there with us. We are all a family now and the people in this company need to know that." She sounded determined. "Besides, Jerry and I need your support."

The three limousines arrived at four o'clock. Jerry's parents went in the first one with Cassie and Jerry. His siblings and their spouses rode in the second and the McAllisters and Latimers rode in the third. It was a twenty minute ride and everyone was excited as they drove up to the front entrance of the Granger Hotel.

The manager of the hotel was there to greet Cassie and Jerry and guided them to the large ballroom on the ground floor.

"Welcome Mrs. Anscott Sanders, Mr. Sanders. I'm Roger Pendergast, the manager. It's an honor to have you here at our hotel. If there is anything you see that is lacking, please let me know and I will see to it immediately."

Everyone followed behind. The view of the foyer, decorated magnificently, was breathtaking.

"This is very beautiful, Mr. Pendergast," Cassie said as she looked around. "I'm sure everything will be fine. However, if there should be something, please tell my personal assistant Glenda, to see to it." Cassie turned and waved for Glenda to join her.

"I know Mrs. Latimer well, Mrs. Anscott Sanders. We've worked on this together for many weeks," he said as he looked at Glenda with a smile. "The receiving line will be right here." He pointed to a place just a few feet away from the entrance. There are some chairs should the ladies feel the need to sit down."

"Where is the dining room?" Cassie asked him.

"The other ballroom for the dinner is just down the hallway. The large door connecting the two will be drawn open at eight o'clock for dinner." He pointed to one of the walls. "If you wish to inspect it I will be glad to show it to you."

"That won't be necessary, Mr. Pendergast. I'm sure it will be equally as beautiful." Cassie gave him a big smile. "We are very pleased, aren't we, Jerry?"

He looked at her with a smile, "I'm overwhelmed, sweetheart. This is fit for a king, isn't it, Mom and Dad?" He turned to his parents. "I guess, you two will stand right next to me when the guests arrive."

"Heavens have mercy, I think I'm going to faint in the middle of this splendor," Claire said to her husband. "I don't think I've ever seen anything like it." She turned to Jerry. "Honey, we'll be right here with you, don't you worry." She squeezed his hand and gave him a reassuring smile. She looked very nice in her long, solid blue dress with a simple silver chain and matching earrings. Cassie had given her some of her mother's jewelry to wear for the evening. Her hair was done in a fancy style and made her look younger, thanks to the fashion consultant's efforts before they left. She had touched up her make-up as well, and the family was astonished at the classy, beautiful woman that emerged when she came down the stairs.

"There you are, Mark," Cassie said as she saw Mark Lenhart and his wife walk in. "I want you two to stand in the receiving line with us. May I introduce Jerry's family to you?" Mark and his wife shook everyone's hand. He looked very pleased to be part of the line.

"It is wonderful to meet all of you. Cassie has told us a lot about you." He sounded polite and took his place next to Claire and Michael at the end of the line.

As the guests began to arrive, Jerry was nervous at first. It took over an hour to shake everyone's hand. Afterwards they mingled with the guests and soon it was time for dinner. At seven-thirty, the big doors opened up to allow a breathtaking view of the fabulously decorated dining room. The crowd let out a murmur of awe as they took their assigned seats around the fifty or so round tables, decorated in white and red roses with lavish greenery arranged to make a tall, dramatic centerpiece. The long head table was at the far side of the room. Cassie and Jerry took their seat and soon everyone looked expectantly toward their table.

Mark Lenhart stood up and welcomed the guests after acknowledging the young couple and the members of the Board of Directors. He led everyone in a toast for Cassie and Jerry and wished them a happy life together. Several other VIP's from different locations along the East coast made appropriate remarks to the young couple. Just when people were getting restless, Mark Lenhart got up and asked Pastor Nathaniel to say a prayer and give thanks for the food.

The five course meal was served flawlessly by a well-trained staff. The Chef had outdone himself with cordon bleu and shrimp as the main course. After the rich dessert of mousse topped with whipped cream was served, another crew came and cleared the tables. Waiters arrived and took orders for whatever the guests wanted to drink.

Finally, Cassie got up and walked up to the podium. She looked stunning in her crème colored, long dress. It was cut in Grecian style with one shoulder free, with a narrow waist and folds of shimmering, silken material hanging perfectly on her slender figure. She looked every bit as classy as her mother.

"Ladies and Gentlemen, thank you for coming to celebrate with me my new life with my husband Jerry. As all of you know, I have been through a horrendous time over the past year and a half. I would like to lift my glass in honor of my parents and my brother Marten. I still miss them terribly and wish they were here to celebrate with us." She took her glass and held it out to the crowd. Everyone got up and lifted their glasses toward her. After all were seated again, Cassie continued.

"Anscott Research Laboratories will continue under the able leadership of Mark Lenhart for now until I'm able to take over in a few years. My father would definitely approve of this arrangement, since he had put his trust in Mark for many years. Together, we will not only see that the company will do well, but look into the possibilities of expansion. It is time we branch out to California and the Midwest. Some of you have wanted to do that for a long time. Now is the moment, as Mark and I, together with the Board, will consider our options." There was enthusiastic applause throughout the room.

She looked at Jerry with a warm smile and then at the audience. "I know you didn't come here to hear about business, but to look over my husband Jerry. The best way for you to get to know him, is for me to let him talk to you and tell you about himself." She waved for Jerry to come to the podium. "He is the best thing that's ever happened to me. Please give him a big hand as he joins me."

Jerry got up with his usual boyish grin and gave her a kiss. The crowd applauded politely.

He took the microphone.

He looked at the crowd and then at Cassie and leaned his tall, lanky body over the podium with a big smile. After a second of silence, he said, "Thanks for joining Cassie and me for this small, humble gathering." A few people laughed. "Now that you've seen me, we can all go home." He grinned at Cassie and pretended to walk away. More started to laugh. She grabbed his arm and pulled him back.

"See, I'm well trained already," he said when he got back to the microphone. The crowd was delighted. After they quieted down, he looked at them and said, "My father said something to me today that put all this into perspective. Just remember son," he told me just before we got here, "they have to be nice to you. You're married to the boss and they're not."

The crowd broke out in laughter and clapped. Jerry just stood there and grinned at them with his usual boyish charm.

"I cannot tell you I quite fit into this crowd," he went on when things calmed down. "But I can tell you that I love this lady." He pointed to Cassie. "My entire wardrobe consisted of jeans and t-shirts before I met her." He pointed at himself. "Now look at me, I do clean up nice." The crowd roared with laughter when he pulled on his expensive jacket in mock pride. "She made me promise I wouldn't complain about these fine threads," he said when they stopped. Straightening himself up, he went on. "Just in case some of you are worried, I don't want to work at Anscott Research Laboratories. Cassie has that well under control. I was and still am the IT manager at Bellami Trucking for as long as they'll have me." A sheepish grin crossed his face. "I will let you in on a secret. I don't make quite as much as she does." They were laughing, some of them with relief.

He draped his lanky, tall frame over the podium again and went on with a mischievous smile. "I want to tell you about our first date." The room grew perfectly still in an instant. "First of all, I was late picking her up. My old car tried to give up the ghost on the way. Then we were too late for the dinner reservation, because the darn thing tried to die several more times before we got to the restaurant. We ended up at Mister Burger so we wouldn't miss the movie." The audience was laughing. "The next date we had, she suggested we might better take her car if we ever wanted to make it anywhere." The crowd loved it. "But we didn't get to the restaurant that time either, since I asked her to come and visit my parents instead. Since it was dinner time, my mom asked her to set the table and help with the dishes afterwards before she knew who Cassie was." With a broad grin he pointed to the lavishly set tables. "As you can see, she learned a lot from my mom how to do it." It took a while before the laughter stopped and he could continue. "I told her she didn't have to do dishes tonight."

Cassie was looking at him with adoration as he continued.

"My dad told her, he thought she would probably make a good secretary at Anscott Research Laboratories." Jerry looked at his parents with a loving smile and blew them a kiss. Claire was embarrassed, but smiled and his dad just sat with a little half grin. The crowd was clapping and cheering and someone roared, "We want to hear more." At that the room was filled with "More, more!"

"I want you to know since we got married, she has bought me some real nice clothes. I like them as long as they hang in the closet and I can still wear my jeans and t-shirts. For some reason, it makes her feel better to know I have them."

Cassie ran up to him and put her hand over his mouth to stop him from talking. He simply took her in his arms and kissed her. The people stood up, laughing, cheering and clapping. Jerry took Cassie's hand and they stood at the podium, smiling at each other and waving to the audience. When the furor died down, Cassie took the microphone and said with a beaming smile, "Now you know why I married him." The room went wild after that. They would have loved him if he had shown up in jeans and a t-shirt.

The limousine took Latimer and Glenda home after the dinner was over. They did not stay when everyone rushed up to Jerry and shook his hand with great enthusiasm. He had completely won them over.

"I don't think it could have gone better," Glenda said as she sank down on the couch with a sigh when they got home. I think Jerry stole the show."

"That boy took that snobbish, skeptical crowd by storm with his simple, friendly honesty and his priceless sense of humor. It was pure genius," Latimer said. "It was also one of the nicest occasions I've ever been to in every way, thanks in part to your organizational talents, lady." He leaned over and kissed her. "You are truly good at what you do."

Chapter 12

Monday morning came soon enough. Latimer was on his way to his office. It was a cold, blustery day as he made his way through heavy traffic.

He would spend the morning going over the notes and interviews Sue Ellen had typed up for him. It was time to re-evaluate the case and decide where to go from here. As always, he found it hard to leave out the personal feelings for the people involved and consider only the facts. He would love to have Allan and Patricia Hellman arrested, put in jail and have someone throw the keys away. The thought, they might inherit fifty million dollars, went against every fiber of his being. He knew feelings like these did nothing to help him figure out who murdered William and Henry. Scientific and circumstantial facts were what counted. It would take this concentrated, objective evaluation to produce the kind of results he needed to solve the case.

Sue Ellen was sitting at her desk. Latimer could smell the coffee brewing.

"Good morning, sunshine," he greeted her with a smile.

"Ain't we in a good mood, Latimer darlin," she said, looking up from her typing. "I came in early because I didn't finish all your recordings."

"Just give me what you have. I want to go over all of them today. I might need your input when you're done."

She was always pleased when he asked her to give her opinion. Sue Ellen, in spite of her southern ways, was intelligent and a keen observer of people and their actions. She had a down- to-earth logic and common sense that had helped Latimer make sense out of a case on several occasions.

"How did the big party go Saturday? That is one shindig I would have loved to have gone to." She had a dreamy expression on her face.

"Sue Ellen, it was the swankiest party I've ever been to. Cassie's new husband Jerry was a hit. He gave a speech that blew them away and they couldn't do enough afterwards to gush over him."

"What did he say that was so great?" She sounded skeptical.

"He told them about their first date and how his old car broke down. In other words, he didn't 'put on airs' as you would say, but he was himself. They loved it. Cassie was so proud of him."

"I declare, maybe I would have been a big hit too, if I'd been invited?" She smiled.

"I have no doubt about that. How did your date with Wayne go?"

"We're doing great."

"I'm happy for you. Is it getting serious?" he asked.

"I think so, we'll see. You can't ever tell about a guy until you've snatched him. It's like a bass nibbling on a worm. You ain't got him until you've reeled him in."

"I am sure he thinks you're the prettiest worm he's ever nibbled on, Sue Ellen." Latimer was laughing as he sat behind his desk, with most of the typed reports in hand. He took out the ones from the interview with the five Hellman children and looked at them one by one.

There was William, the doctor, a mature, responsible and educated man, who seemingly had no need for his father's money. However, there was a deep-seated resentment in him, because of his father's criticism of not spending enough time with his family. Did he not do exactly what he learned from the man who made lots of money at the expense of building a relationship with his wife and children? William had tried to impress his dad by becoming a neurosurgeon, yet his father did not appreciate any of it and continued to ignore him.

Latimer was sure, that was not reason enough to murder him. He put William's report away and took out Grant's. What a likable, handsome and lovable scoundrel. Out of the need to be noticed, he squandered his life on childish pranks fit for a teenager. Grant Hellman never grew past the teenage stage, until he heard his father's remarks on the tape. However, he was the only one of the five to take to heart what he heard him say. Latimer couldn't help but notice his intelligence and self-assurance. He could, if necessary, hide behind this reasonable and positive reaction, to cover up the fact he had murdered his father, because he needed the money. Deep inside, Latimer hoped it wasn't so, because he liked him best of all.

The next file was about Sylvia, a product of a life of rejection by the men she loved. First there was her father and then the man who left her a day before the wedding. She had desired nothing more than to trust and love both men, but both replaced her with something or someone else. Her father gave money to many people and organizations, but not to her. Her fiancé humiliated her publicly by leaving her and replacing her with her money. She had built a wall of hatred for men around her that might never be broken, and could very well have led to her murdering her father. To kill Henry could be seen as necessary. Some pain can only be tolerated by inflicting pain on others, when forgiveness is absent. She was intelligent and definitely capable of pulling it off.

Latimer wondered what Sylvia was alluding to when she mentioned she had gotten along just fine without her father's money. Her plush condo proved it. He made a note to look into that.

The two youngest children of the clan were, without doubt, the most spoiled. Becky, with her stunning, good looks and innocent ditsy blond act, could easily pull off the murder of her father. The fact, she was also an alcoholic, didn't hurt. With her lavish lifestyle, she was no doubt constantly short of money. She was a born actress and had not only fooled her father, but most of the men she met, to give her what she wanted. They became expendable when no longer needed. Her father was simply one of them. In time he became worth more dead than alive as her expenses increased, yet his allowance did not.

Latimer reached for Allan's folder. Sue Ellen had just finished typing it. Here was a person one loved to hate. Latimer closed his eyes and envisioned Brighton putting handcuffs on him and reading him his Miranda rights. The boy was a sociopath, someone with no feelings of right or wrong, or concern for the well-being of others. Whatever felt good, that was good in his mind. Whatever was bad for him, it was bad. Years ago, Latimer had caught a murderer just like Allan. The court psychiatrist had explained to the jury, that people like that suffered from a brain abnormality that made it impossible to think about anyone but their own feelings. Since that part of the brain was dead so to speak, there was no hope for rehabilitation for those with that affliction.

Could it be that Allan was one of those murderers? His lack of sorrow over his father's death or the absence of concern for Henry as a human being certainly put him into the realm of being the perfect suspect.

There was one more folder to look at. Patricia Hellman. Latimer didn't include her as a suspect, but her willingness to turn her own kids in as possible murderers put her in a special category all its own. Either she was insane or deluded to think they'd get off, because she had a lot of money. On the other hand, stranger things have happened in the history of the court system. There could be no doubt, money does talk.

He wondered if Henry had known more than just the existence of the tape. After all, there wasn't that much on it to warrant murdering him. He definitely wanted to talk to him, judging from that phone call.

Latimer looked at some notes he had made. One of the people he hadn't interviewed yet was Grace Harriett, Mr. Hellman's secretary. He left her fifty-thousand dollars.

"Sue Ellen, do me a favor and call Grace Harriett, Hellman's secretary. She should be on the list Gary Norton gave me. Also, Karl Rockwell, a friend who got twenty-thousand. I need to interview them both."

"Will do, Latimer darlin," she said with a cheerful voice.

Latimer thought about William Carl Hellman. He was a good man, successful and generous, a faithful husband and father, who tried so very hard to instill in his children a solid work ethic. He tried even harder to live up to what he believed in, to love God and his neighbors, namely the poor and needy in the community. How is it, he could fail so miserably with his children? Not only did they not grow up to be self-sufficient, but embraced a philosophy of dependency on his money. In spite of showing them by example how to give to others, he failed to give freely of his love by spending time with them or giving them his individual attention. The only thing they saw was, he had plenty of was money, which he freely shared with everyone else, but them. In the end, that is all they wanted, since they couldn't have his approval. His last video put the last nail in his coffin. With his last words, he once again showed them where they had failed first, instead of how much he loved them. What a tragic family in spite of the millions.

Latimer thought about Cassie and Jerry. Would they treat their children the same or would they understand, it is not money that turns kids into balanced adults? He hoped they would understand, what children need, is parents who show them love by spending time with them every day. Love and discipline go hand in hand. All William Hellman showed his children was discipline, while Patricia showed them only what she perceived as love, which was in truth mere indulgence.

Latimer wondered what kind of a father he would have made. He cringed as he remembered the many hours he left his wife Mary alone, because of his work. Raising children was not an easy thing to do if one wanted to do it right, he thought. He was sort of glad they couldn't have any.

"You have an appointment with Grace Harriett this afternoon at three," Sue Ellen shouted from her desk. "She lives not too far from here." Latimer nearly jumped off his chair as her powerful voice shook him out of his reverie.

"Sue Ellen, sweetheart, you don't have to shout. I can hear you just fine."

"Ok," she shouted back.

He had to smile. There was no one quite like her.

On his way to Grace Harriett's apartment, he called Glenda.

"Everybody is so excited and pleased about Jerry," she told him. "He was a smash hit last Saturday. Cassie is absolutely delighted how he handled the whole thing. Even his family was extremely well received. I really think it will be easier on both of them now that he can be himself and nobody has to worry about appearances or rumors." Glenda sounded pleased. "Jerry showed up at her office this morning. You would've thought a rock star had arrived. Everybody wanted to shake his hand and talk to him. He just put on that silly grin and all the women were instantly smitten." She laughed. "Needless to say, he was in jeans."

"I just wanted to let you know I will be home early today. I have an appointment at three and then I'll take some work home with me and sit by the fireplace and warm up."

"You're not getting sick, are you, honey?" She sounded worried.

"No, since I'm self-employed now, I can afford to do that," he said with a certain satisfaction in his voice. "I got to go, I'm at my destination. I'll see you tonight."

Grace Harriett's apartment was at the top floor of a renovated brownstone. He rang the doorbell and was let in by a buzzer.

"Please come in, Mr. Latimer. I've been wondering if anyone was going to talk to me about Mr. Hellman's murder." She was a middle-aged woman with a short, curly hair cut. She was quite overweight, but hid it well with a loose-fitting top over expensive looking slacks. Her face was round and friendly with brown eyes and a small nose. "Come on in. I have made us a pot of coffee. In this terrible weather, I'm sure you can use it."

"It is nice of you to see me, Mrs. Harriett. Please call me Latimer, everybody does."

"Thanks, Latimer, please call me Grace. I've heard so much about you from Pat Hellman and Allan. They have kept me informed about what's going on."

"Are you still working in your job, Grace?"

"No, I'm not. It will be hard for me to find something at my age. The money I got from his Will helps me a lot." She brought out two mugs of steaming coffee and put them down on the table in front of the couch. The living room was small, but tastefully decorated in contemporary furniture. Everything was neat and clean.

"Did you know you were going to inherit something, Grace?" Latimer asked.

"No, I didn't. It came as a complete surprise. Then again, Mr. Hellman was truly a nice gentleman. He didn't deserve such ungrateful children. I always knew they were after his money." He sensed she felt strongly about that.

"I gather you didn't like any of them?"

"I didn't. Especially Allan and Sylvia treated me like I didn't exist when they came to see him. It felt very demeaning. Grant was different. He was charming and outgoing and would talk to me. But I knew he always showed up when he was in trouble or wanted money."

"Did Mr. Hellman give it to him?" Latimer asked.

"Sometimes he would, but not often. That's when Patricia would get involved and the fighting would begin." She looked at Latimer, suddenly embarrassed. "I don't know why I'm telling you this. You must think me a gossip." She took a sip of her coffee. "I really liked Mr. Hellman and I'm convinced one of his kids killed him." She was close to tears.

"You loved him, didn't you, Grace?" Latimer spoke softly.

The remark took her totally by surprise.

"How did you know? He never did." She sat with her hands folded in her lap, her eyes lowered.

"It's alright, Grace. No one will ever hear it from me." Latimer said gently. "I'm sure he didn't know."

"He would never have done anything improper even if he had known, Latimer. He lived what he preached." She looked up at him with relief. "I certainly never told him." She relaxed visibly. "I remember the day he told me about how he changed from a ruthless investor to a Christian by listening to a Billy Graham Crusade in a hotel room in Miami, years ago. He said he fell to his knees and accepted Christ into his heart. That one action changed his life dramatically and he started giving to charities, helping the homeless and many people in need. It was his greatest heartache that neither his wife nor his children ever wanted any part of his faith. I'm sorry he died without ever seeing them change."

"Did you listen to him, Grace?" Latimer asked.

"Yes, I did. I started going to the same church he went to. We had many wonderful talks about God and that's when I fell in love with him. I would have never told him or do anything to come between him and his wife. He had no idea I felt that way about him." She sat back in her chair and sighed. "It has kept me from ever getting interested in anyone else, although he encouraged me to do so many times."

"How long did you work for him?"

"Fifteen years in all. At first he had an office in the city and I worked there for him as one of several secretaries. When he retired, he had his office at the estate and chose me to go with him."

"Does that mean you had access to the entire house?"

"Yes, I could come and go as I pleased. To the rest of the family I was simply another one of the hired help."

"Tell me about when he was still active. Did you and he travel a lot?"

"We travelled to many places because of his business. He always insisted that Patricia went with him as well. She enjoyed it and was there for most business trips. They had a nanny and a housekeeper and she was free to go with him."

"Did they have a good marriage?" Latimer asked.

"At first, when I started working for him, they did. Later, they fought about the kids and money. It was strange. When they were travelling they enjoyed each other more. It was as if Pat was a different person when she was away from those horrible kids. She was loving and kind and didn't nag at him constantly about giving them more money." She got up. "Would you like another cup of coffee?"

"No, thank you, I'm fine," Latimer said. "Can you tell me which of the kids you think might be capable of murdering Mr. Hellman?"

"That would be difficult to say, since all of them have enough selfishness in them to do it. If I had to choose one, though, it would be Allan or maybe even Sylvia. Both of them have a meanness that is frightening. Allen has no thought for anyone but himself. Sylvia, because she hates men and that included her father, has the smarts and toughness to pull it off. None of the others hated him. They just didn't like him very much, because of the way he restricted their income."

"Did you suspect at any time that he was being poisoned?"

"No. I did hear him say to me several times during the last few months of his life that he didn't trust his kids. He never told me he thought one of them would murder him, though. The first time I heard that, was on the video."

Latimer got up.

"You've been most helpful, Grace. Thank you for giving me so much valuable information." He turned to her before he went out the door. "You did hear that Henry, the butler, was poisoned in the same way as Mr. Hellman?"

She held on to the doorframe.

"Oh my goodness, nobody bothered to tell me. That is terrible. He was such a wonderful, faithful man. I'm so sorry to hear that." She looked at Latimer with sudden determination. "I do hope you catch whoever did this and put them away for a long time."

Latimer looked at her with a half-smile as she closed the door behind him.

Late that same afternoon he had an appointment with Karl Rockwell at his home. The man and his wife lived in a modest neighborhood on the outskirts of town. The house was much larger than the rest and well kept. An older woman opened the door.

"Come on in, Mr. Latimer. Karl is expecting you." She led him into the back of the house into the family room. From what little he could see, the rest of the house was immaculately clean. The furniture consisted of a hodgepodge of antiques, probably passed down from the family. A small dog of questionable heritage came running up to Latimer, his tail wagging furiously.

"Be careful of my big killer attack dog, he'll lick you to death," a large man with white hair and a full beard said as he got up from his chair. "I'm Karl Rockwell and this is my wife Angela. Welcome to our home." He had a wonderful, warm smile as he held out his hand to

Latimer. "Have a seat and make yourself at home. Angela will bring you some coffee. It's the only thing that'll help you feel better in this terrible weather."

Latimer sat down and looked around the comfortable, warm surroundings. A roaring fire added to the cozy atmosphere.

"Thank you for seeing me, Mr. Rockwell," he said.

"Please call us Karl and Angela, Mr. Latimer," his wife said as she sat his coffee cup in front of him.

"Then you must call me Latimer, everybody does," he said as he took the cup.

"I can imagine why you're hear, Latimer," Karl said. "That was some Will William put together. I can't say I blame him. With his kids the way they are, I wasn't surprised," he added.

"Were you his close friend, Karl?"

"We knew each other for forty years. William and I met at a conference in Miami. Later on, he, Patricia, Angela and I spent a lot of time together on many occasions for thirty of those years. The last ten years our relationship dwindled to just William and I. Patricia acted more distant the more successful William became. She sought out people of her elevated status." Karl said.

"In other words, she became a snob," Angela added with a smile. "Let's put it the way it was."

"Did either of you suspect any one of his children could kill him?" Latimer asked.

"I did," Angela answered before Karl could say anything. "They are the most selfish, disgusting kids that poor man could've ever asked for. There was nothing he did for them, they appreciated. I'm glad we are not wealthy. That way our children won't have to fight over our money like his have been." She sounded upset. "He was a wonderful, generous and kind man, who didn't deserve to be killed by his horrible family."

"Which of the children do you think could have done it, Angela?" Latimer asked.

"Every one of them, but if I had to pick just one, Allan comes to mind," she said without hesitation.

"Angie, you shouldn't judge so easily." He turned to Latimer. "We don't know. I don't think William, the oldest, is capable of doing it. He is a steady, hard working man in his own right and doesn't need his dad's money. Grant has been wild, but his antics were more or less rebellion to gain attention. Sylvia has a good heart deep down, but because she was so hurt, she puts on this hard outer layer of defense. If I had to choose, Becky or Allan would be the ones. There is something very wrong with them. It is deeper than just wanting money. They are what I refer to as bad seed."

Latimer was astounded at his insight.

"What was your occupation, Karl," Latimer asked.

"I was VP at a local bank in Glenridge. William had an account with us for many years and I took care of it. I watched him, as he increased his wealth, from a few thousand to a few hundred million dollars over the years. He was a very smart investor. His wealth never changed our friendship."

"It sure changed Patricia," Angela interjected. "She definitely let us know, without coming right out, we were not quite fit for her crowd in the last few years."

"I don't know if she meant it that way, but her social circle was on a different level than what we were used to," Karl said. "Eventually, we lost touch with her. William would come over by himself many times and we would sit around the fire with a good cigar and talk about old times. That's when he would share about his family. He was very worried and unhappy with all of them, including Patricia." Karl looked at Latimer with sadness. "He was not able to pass on his values to them, and he knew it."

"We went to see him when he got sick," Angela said. "It was awful. He knew he was dying and asked us what he could do to reach his kids." She wiped her eyes. "What could we do? We knew how they were. They couldn't wait for him to die and get his money."

"Did he ever say anything about one of his children would murder him?" Latimer asked.

"No, not to us. We were astounded when we heard about it that day at the lawyer's office." Karl said.

"It was horrible and it broke our hearts," Angela said.

"I wish he had told us. I would have done something about it." Karl sounded angry.

"What would you have done, Karl?" Latimer asked.

"I don't know, I would have thought of something." He was thoughtful. "I have the strange feeling, William didn't want to do anything, because he felt he had failed his family in spite of all his money."

They sat in silence for a long time.

Chapter 13

The weather wasn't any better the next morning. It was February and summer seemed an eternity away. Latimer was on his way to the precinct to discuss with the technicians what they found out about the tape. From what Brighton said, they had found something interesting in the local lab. It would hopefully be confirmed when the report came back from the copy they sent to New York.

Brighton was waiting for him in his office.

"The technician in the lab called me and said they found something interesting. He is ready for us, let's go. I wonder what it is. I could use a break. I haven't gotten anywhere with Henry Gossomer's case." He sounded discouraged.

"Don't worry. Mine and yours are connected. We'll solve them together, just like the last time." Latimer sounded a lot more confident than he felt.

"This is Tom Specter, Latimer. He worked on the tape," Brighton said. "What did you find, Tom?"

"It's not a high quality tape, that's for sure, but I worked with it for quite a while, until I think I got something." He turned to the computer. "I transferred the whole thing on here so we can work with it easier."

Latimer and Brighton stood behind him and watched as the footage appeared. It seemed much clearer and brighter. When they got to the dark figure, Tom put it on pause.

"You see this figure? I asked the computer to tell me if it is a man or a woman by the configuration of the body parts. It told me it's a woman. There are no facial features available for the computer to work with. I'm sure it helps you guys to know that the perp is female."

"I hate to put a damper on things, Tom," Latimer said. "Allan Hellman is built like a woman. He is slender, with small bones and delicate features. At least this eliminates Grant and William from the bunch. That leaves the two girls and Allan." He turned to Tom. "Can you tell us if the person was tall or short?"

"Not from the angle where the camera was. The dimensions are distorted in such a way, it is impossible to tell. Maybe the lab in New York can give you that information."

"This is great, Tom. We appreciate all your effort. It gives us something to work with," Latimer said. "We have narrowed it from five to three. That's pretty good."

On the way to Brighton's office, Harold Brown came out of a door just as they passed it.

"Hi Harold, how are things going?" Latimer said with a friendly smile.

"Latimer, it's good to see you," Inspector Brown answered. His smile never reached his eyes. "Checking us out again, are you?"

"I guess so, Harold." He was truly sorry about their rift, but could not see what he could do to change the man's attitude towards him, after solving a case he had given up on.

When they got to Brighton's office, Latimer sat in front of the desk with a cup of coffee in hand.

"Which one of the women do you think it could be?" Brighton asked.

"I'm going to talk to them again," Latimer said. "I want to find out where Sylvia gets her money to live the way she does. I don't think it's a man. She hates all men. From what her sister Becky told me, she doesn't get enough monthly income to afford her high lifestyle. She was pretty flippant about her father not giving her a big allowance. Something is going on we don't know about." , get me an appointment with Sylvia Hellman as soon as you can."

"Will do, boss," she said. "Are you coming back to the office before lunch? I have to go to the doctor for my yearly check-up at one."

"I can be there by then," he said. "Brighton and I will go to lunch if he's free." He hung up and looked up. "You are free, aren't you?"

"Sure, if you're paying." Brighton flashed his brightest smile.

"It's a deal. Where do you want to go? When we get there, I'll tell you about the fabulous party Glenda and I went to last Saturday."

"Let's do Chinese, Latimer. That way I can eat as much as I want."

"I forgot how much it takes to fill up your lanky frame, Kid."

To his surprise, Sylvia Hellman agreed to see him today at four in the afternoon. Latimer arrived at her condo in plenty of time to chat with the doorman.

"I bet you don't get too many visitors in this terrible weather," he said in a casual tone.

"You'd be surprised how many people get out in the worst storm. In my line of work, I see all kinds." He was happy to have someone to talk to.

"Does Ms. Hellman get a lot of visitors?"

"I'm not supposed to say, but since you're one of her friends, I guess I can tell you. I remember you when you came before." He looked around to see if anyone else was there. "She is a classy lady and gets a lot of clients coming at all times."

"Really?"

"Oh yes, I know some of them."

"You couldn't tell me who they are?" Latimer had no idea what the man was talking about.

"Oh no. In her line of work you don't want everyone to know."

"In her line of work?" Latimer held his breath.

"Aren't you here for your diet regimen?"

"Of course I am. It's working real well, too. Have you tried it?" Latimer was really fishing this time.

"I can't afford that stuff. I hear it's very expensive." The man looked at his substantial belly. "I could sure use it."

Latimer looked at his watch.

"I better go up. I don't want to be late. You know how she is about that."

"She's a tough one alright."

So she was into high-end health supplements, combined with personal, dietary counseling. Latimer was amazed how easy it was to get information from people. One bored doorman was a veritable encyclopedia on the business dealings of Sylvia Hellman. The strange thing was the man would have sworn he didn't give away a thing.

"Please, come on in. I don't have but fifteen minutes to talk to you. I have an appointment after that." She waved him in.

"I appreciate you seeing me. With all your clients I'm sure you are a busy lady."

"What do you know about my clientele?" Her tone was sharp.

"I'm a private detective, Ms. Hellman. I get paid to know things." He looked at her with a twinkle in his eyes. "Maybe I should try some of your supplements." He patted his stomach. "I sure I could use them"

She suddenly relaxed.

"I don't think you can afford them, Mr. Latimer." She waved him in to take a seat in the living room. "I make enough money on my own, without my father's help, as you can see."

"Wasn't that what he wanted all of his children to do?" Latimer asked. "From where I sit, you are doing exactly what he knew you were capable of doing, if he stopped giving you any more money. You made it on your own. Did you ever tell him how well you did, Ms. Hellman? He would've been pleased."

"I never talked to him again after my fiancé left me. I was too embarrassed." She looked sad. "Now I wish I had."

"I remember on the video, he said you were the intelligent one, the one most like him. In other words, you have what it takes to succeed, just like he did." Latimer looked around the room. "You are doing it."

"I never thought about it. All I ever remembered him telling me was, I ran after the wrong man and squandered all my money." She sat in the chair and fumbled with a tissue. "I have spent a lot of time thinking about that video he made for us since I talked to you last. He looked so sad, thinking that one of us would kill him." She looked at Latimer with profound sadness as she went on. "I wish I had listened to him. Looking back, I know he wanted only the best for all of us. He knew I had gotten terribly hurt and took it out on him. He tried several times to get in touch with me, but I hung up on him each time." She was crying. "I wish I had never heard that video. The hardest thing on there was that he asked all of us to forgive him. We are the ones who should have asked his forgiveness. He did only what any good father would do. He tried to prepare his children to stand on their own two feet."

"I can't tell you how proud he would be, if he could hear you now, Sylvia. It is not too late to ask him to forgive you. It will help you heal. Your father knew about forgiveness, because God had forgiven him and accepted him many years ago. Remember, what he told you about his faith. Try to do what he did and give your life over to the One your father trusted, Jesus Christ. Then you can start over again to rebuild your life without the hatred and distrust of all men. We are not all the same, Sylvia. Look at your dad. He was good, kind and generous and loved you very much." Latimer leaned back in his chair, stunned at what just happened. He came here to find a killer and found a woman, ready to make peace with her father.

The doorbell rang. Sylvia jumped up from her chair.

"Oh my goodness, I forgot my next client." She looked at Latimer and suddenly reached around his neck and hugged him. "You are the best detective I've ever met," she said as she wiped the remnant of her tears away. "I will call you if I hear anything that might help you," she said on the way to the front door.

He let himself out without saying another word as a heavy set woman walked in.

Latimer walked up to the elevator. He was amazed. Of all the things he would have ever expected today, Sylvia Hellman wanting to turn her life around wasn't one of them. Now he understood why she agreed so readily to talk to him. He suddenly realized, it was the second of the five children who had been touched by the video in a special way. Maybe Grant was not trying to con him, but was truly ready to change his life as well.

It would be interesting to see what the rest of them will do. He couldn't fathom Becky or Allan suddenly changing their selfish behavior any time soon, and had no idea what William really thought. He had learned to hide his feelings well as a physician.

Latimer had only a short way to reach his condo. Glenda was not home yet. He sat in his favorite chair and decided to keep what had happened to himself. He was sure Sylvia expected privacy and he would give it to her.

His cell rang. It was Glenda. She told him she would be late and not to wait with dinner. She had an important meeting to go to with Cassie and they would eat there. He had not been alone in the evening in a long time and actually enjoyed it as he rummaged around the refrigerator for something to eat. After a while a tuna sandwich sounded good. It reminded him of his bachelor days. Some of Glenda's healthy chips would go well with it.

His thoughts turned to Becky for some reason. He knew she was an alcoholic and emotionally unstable, but that didn't make her a murderer. Somehow, in spite of her talk of how she used men, he agreed with her father, that she was equally used by them. There was something vulnerable and defenseless about her. It wasn't her looks alone, but her phony bravado in her decision to remain unmarried. In the end, it left her alone in life, since her family was not exactly there for her. Even her mother concentrated her affections on Allan to a point, it left Becky outside the inner circle.

  Latimer tried hard to figure Patricia out. She was a woman of many contradictions, unpredictable and unstable, fighting fiercely for her children's financial wellbeing. He could not detect a deep love in her for anyone, though, in spite of it. It was more a control issue. As long as she held the purse strings, they would always love her. Latimer, the more he got to know her, the more he disliked her. She was every bit as selfish and self-centered as her children in his opinion. She definitely controlled Allan, a boy in a man's body.

  Latimer wondered what each one would do, when they finally received the fifty million dollars inheritance. Wealth like that brings out the true character of a person. Would William continue to work or give up his medical profession? Latimer didn't think so. He had too much invested in it, with years of study as well as the prestige of being known as a neurosurgeon.

  Would Grant change his life, go to college and become an investment broker like his father, or continue his life with women and fast cars?

  He was sure Sylvia would expand her business and make it big in whatever she chose to do. She still had something to prove to her father and make him proud of her.

  Latimer was afraid, Becky would become a hopeless alcoholic and end up in despair and degradation in spite of her millions. In the end, she would squander it on men and lose her soul in the process.

  He could not guess what Allan would do. He could continue to hang on his mother's apron strings or cut loose and go wild to make up for lost time. If he was on drugs, like Patricia said, there was very little hope he would ever straighten out his life.

  Latimer still had no idea, which one of these five people murdered their father and the butler. When the report from the lab in New York came in to show what kind of poison it was, it was time to find out how they obtained it and where. There was nothing he could do but wait until then. He suddenly remembered the burnt paper in the fireplace in Mr. Hellman's bedroom. Henry said it was Patricia who messed up the room. What did she burn that was so important? Latimer was sure it was something to hide from him and the police to protect one of her children. He wondered if she knew who committed the murders. Not for one minute did he believe she told the truth when she accused Allan and Becky in a round about way. It had to be a ruse. Yet he couldn't figure out what it could possibly be.

The dynamics of this family were complicated, to say the least. The only one who was, what one could call normal, was the victim and his butler. They must've talked to each other over the last few months. Henry could've been a great source of information in this case. Latimer was sorry he was gone. To think he gave his life for people who did in no way appreciate all he had done for so many years, was sad.

Latimer was sitting in the dark when Glenda walked in.

"Are you ok, honey?" she asked. "It's completely dark in here." She turned on a light.

"I was going over my case and didn't realize it. I'm glad you're home. How did your meeting go?"

"It was long and boring, but necessary. That's the way these things usually are. Cassie handles herself quite well for her age and lack of experience. She was born to do this. A lot of the managers are starting to respect her."

Glenda put her briefcase on the little table by the front door and took her coat off. "It's wet and nasty out there," she said as she sat on the arm of his chair. "This is better than a fireplace." She snuggled up close to him and laid her head on his shoulder. "It's still wonderful to come home to you, handsome," she said as she kissed him. "How did your day go?"

Latimer smiled and thought about Sylvia.

"I had a surprisingly great day."

"Do you want to talk about it?" Glenda asked.

"No, I just want to sit here and enjoy being with you, sweetheart. What we have together is amazing. Two people finding real love at our age. I don't think that happens very often."

"I feel like we've known each other forever. It'll keep us both young," she said with a smile. "Then again, getting old with someone like you isn't such a terrible thought either."

Chapter 14

Another week had gone by and Latimer still hadn't heard about the poison from the branch of Anscott Research Laboratories in New York. He was getting impatient and so was the Hellman family. He had several phone calls throughout the week, inquiring how his investigation was going. One was from Gary Norton.

"They are badgering me, Latimer. Is there anything you can tell me that I can pass along as progress?" he had asked just yesterday.

"I'll let you know when I have something," Latimer told him. "You remind me of the Chief at the precinct."

This was the phase he hated, when the case seemed to be going nowhere, and he had no idea who the murderer was. It was the time Brighton would ask, 'Where do we go from here?' To which he would answer, 'Something is going to come up, Kid'.

He was sitting in his office with his first cup of coffee of the morning. Before he came to work, he told Sue Ellen she didn't have to come in today, since there was nothing for her to do. When he called Brighton's office, they told him he was out. The frustrating part was, he had no idea where to go from here. Thinking about the big fee he had already collected, he felt guilty. He should be doing something.

His cell phone rang. It was Pat Christianson from the coroner's office.

"How is my favorite private sleuth this morning?" she said in her low, rough voice. "I have the report from the Anscott Research Laboratories in New York. It's very interesting and thorough. I think you should come by and we'll go over the results together."

He jumped at the chance to get out of the office and was on his way within minutes. Pat sounded positive and maybe this was it, he would be able to get closer to solving the case.

"Come on in handsome." Pat sat in her office with a folder in hand. "This is something I've never run across before. I'm glad we sent it in. There is no way our lab would've ever found out what killed him." She pointed to the chair for Latimer to sit down. "This is some fancy lab. They not only sent the results on paper, but included a CD with more details. I'm impressed. Whoever you know at Anscott Research Laboratories, they must have some pull."

"It's only the owner," Latimer said and smiled.

"That explains it. You seem to have come up in the world since you're on your own. Good for you, I knew you were not ready to retire." She looked at him with new respect and then turned on the computer. "Here it is."

A man in a white coat appeared on the screen.

"My name is Dr. Richard Keller and I'm in charge of the Research Division for the Study of Exotic Poisons. Mrs. Anscott Sanders has requested that we give you a report on our findings of the blood sample you sent to our lab. She instructed us to give one report for a non-physician and another for the coroner. I will start with the explanation for you, Mr. Latimer. You may not remember me, but I was introduced to you at the company event two weeks ago." Latimer was impressed.

"First, let me explain that there are many unknown facts about countless plants and their medicinal properties found in the region of the Amazon River. New discoveries are made almost daily. The natives are a great resource in finding them. Some poisons we have found do not even have names yet. All we know about them, they are highly toxic and therefore extremely deadly. However, taken in minute quantities, they will eventually be beneficial to medical science. The poison we found in the blood sample you sent, is one of those. We would be interested to find out where and how it was found and brought here to the US. Maybe when you solve the case, Mr. Latimer, you can tell us those details.

What we know about this poison is, it was given gradually to your victim. Apparently, the main effect of it is that it paralyzes the involuntary muscles of the body, like the heart. In laymen's terms, it makes it stop. It leaves only a minute residue, undetectable by normal test methods in ninety percent of labs in the country. Without our sophisticated equipment, your coroner's conclusion of a heart failure would be the only possible diagnosis of cause of death. It was administered over several weeks. It means there were no violent symptoms, just an overall feeling of fatigue and gradual decline. The same goes for the second blood sample you sent in. It contained the same poison. However, it was given in a much larger, lethal quantity once or at most twice. In other words, the second victim would have died much sooner and more violently than the first.

I hope this will help you find the murderer, Mr. Latimer. Please don't forget to let us know how they got the poison. We would greatly appreciate it."

"You weren't kidding when you said you knew somebody at Anscott. That's what I call first class connections." Pat Christianson sounded impressed.

"Cassie Anscott is actually a close friend. Glenda works as her personal assistant. You remember the case about her father and brother, don't you?" He asked.

"Of course, how could I forget? Do you have any idea how the poison was brought into the country?" She asked.

"No, but I will definitely try to find out. As a matter of fact, that'll be my next project."

She took out the CD and handed to him.

"This is yours. I have another one. The rest of it is my detailed medical report and wouldn't be of any interest to you, my love." She smiled at him with her usual tease. "How is that gorgeous wife of yours?"

"Glenda is doing fine. I'm a fortunate man to have found her. Thanks, Pat. This will really help me, I hope. Who knows Pat, maybe we are part of a medical breakthrough if we find out where the stuff came from." He got up and walked to the door. "Take care and thanks for all your help." He threw her a kiss before he left.

Back in the car, he called Sylvia Hellman. She agreed to see him this afternoon at two. Then he dialed Patricia's number. She was at home and asked him to come right out since she would be gone this afternoon.

Patricia was in the family room when he got there and greeted him warmly. Looking at her, serene and classy in her stylish, elegant outfit, he found it hard to remember the thoughtless, arrogant woman from a few days ago. He would have to remember how good an actress she was.

"How nice to see you again, Mr. Latimer. It is always a pleasure," she said as she shook his hand and pointed to a chair next to her. "What can I do for you today?"

"I have one simple question for you, Mrs. Hellman. Has anyone in your family ever been to the Amazon River?"

There was a flicker in her eyes before she lowered them. As he watched her closely, he saw the hesitation before she answered.

"I don't think so. I mean, I don't know all the places my children travel to when they go on vacation, but I don't remember any of them mentioning going to the Amazon."

Latimer knew she was lying. She fully understood he was asking about the poison and wasn't about to tell on her children.

"Why are you asking, Mr. Latimer?" she said. Her voice was even, without emotion or fear. "I can't imagine."

"I'm exploring all possibilities, Ma'am. As you can imagine, this is not an easy case and your full co-operation is necessary to find the person who murdered your husband and Henry."

"Are you saying I'm not telling you the truth, Mr. Latimer?" She looked at him with a steady look.

"Yes, I am."

"In that case I would have to ask you to leave my house and don't come back. I'm not part of the Will that says I have to talk to you if I want to inherit. I have my money." She got up and pointed for him to leave. There was real anger in her voice. "You have some nerve accusing me of lying."

"I'm sorry you feel that way, Mrs. Hellman. Protecting your children will not keep me from finding the truth, with or without you." Latimer bowed his head slightly and left.

Before he got to the front door, one of the maids stepped out from behind a door. She put her finger to her mouth for him not to give her away, and waved to follow her outside to a small alcove.

"My name is Margit Lowell. I'm one of the kitchen help. I started working here only four months ago." She was whispering and looked around anxiously.

"What can I do for you, Margit?" Latimer asked in a low voice.

"I need to talk to you about something I heard the other day. This place gives me the creeps."

"I will meet you anywhere you say." Latimer said. He sounded interested.

"I can meet you at Mr. Burger down the street after I get off work at five this afternoon." She looked around nervously. "I can meet you at five-thirty."

"That sounds good. I will be there, Margit." Latimer stepped out of the way as she hurried back into the house."

Latimer got into his car. He was excited. This sounded like a break. He certainly needed one. He thought about Patricia. Her reaction was unusually strong, he thought. He must've hit a nerve. When he got into his car, he called Brighton.

"I have something for you that pertains to your case. Can you come to my office? I have given Sue Ellen the day off and have to stick around. Maybe we can order lunch in."

"That sounds great. I sure could use the help." Brighton sounded cheerful as usual. "I'll be there in fifteen minutes."

Latimer ordered a large pizza. He knew Brighton would have no trouble finishing it off.

"I'm so glad you got me out of my office. I was sitting there with no idea what to do next about my case," he said as he draped his lanky body over the chair in front of Latimer's desk.

"Welcome to my world," Latimer said. "I was in the same boat, until I got a call from the coroner's office this morning. They got the report back from the Anscott Research Laboratory. It confirmed it was an unknown, exotic poison from the Amazon River which attacks the involuntary muscles of the heart. It makes it stop beating and the cause of death looks like heart failure. It was given to Mr. Hellman over several weeks in tiny amounts. Henry got his dose over only two days. He experienced much more pain and discomfort than Hellman before he died."

The outside door opened and the pizza delivery man walked in. Latimer paid him. Brighton ate like he had been starved for days. Latimer smiled as he watched him. He liked the Kid.

"Let's get back to our case. Poor Henry apparently had a pretty violent death. I still don't know what it is he knew other than there was a camera and the video tape." Latimer took another slice of pizza and decided he wouldn't tell Glenda about it.

"How do you think one of the kids got a hold of the poison?" Brighton asked between bites.

"With an unknown poison, like we're dealing with, it had to have been picked up from some native witch doctor in the Amazon jungle. When I asked Patricia if any of the family had ever visited there, she got terribly upset and threw me out of the house."

"Which means, someone had been there and she knows who," Brighton said, taking a fourth slice.

"I had an interesting talk with one of the maids at the Hellman estate. She wants to meet with me later this afternoon. I think she saw or heard something of interest. She sounded really scared."

"That sounds great. We certainly could use a break," Brighton said between bites.

Latimer decided to stop after the third slice and got up to get a refill of his coffee. "Do you want some?" He asked.

"That would be nice, thanks."

"You might as well finish off the pizza. We wouldn't want it to go to waste, would we?" Latimer said with a smile as he pushed the rest of the pizza toward Brighton.

"How would we find out which one of them bought it from a dealer down there?" Brighton asked.

"I don't know yet. Let's just concentrate first on finding out who went down there," Latimer said as he put the coffee in front of him. "I have an appointment with Sylvia this afternoon. I think she'll tell me if she knows."

"You spoil me, Latimer. I used to get coffee for you, remember? It feels weird you doing it," Brighton said, watching him.

"I'm trying to get you to realize you're in charge now and I'm the one following you."

"That's never going to happen and you know it." Brighton gave him his brightest smile as he reached for the last slice. "To me, you'll always be the boss."

Latimer rang the bell of Sylvia Hellman's apartment. Sylvia stood with a glass of carrot juice in her hand and waved him in.

"Come on in, Latimer, how good to see you." She pointed toward the living room and he sat down in the same chair as before.

"Mother called and told me not to talk to you anymore." She smiled.

"Did she say why?" Latimer asked.

"No, but she was pretty upset. What did you do to her, Latimer?" Sylvia was teasing.

"I just asked her one question and she lied to me. I told her she lied and that's when she threw me out." Latimer stroked his beard thoughtfully. "I wonder which one of the children she is protecting."

"What was the question?" Sylvia asked.

"Have any of you been to the Amazon jungle?" He studied her face as he said it.

Sylvia sat down on the couch and looked at him with a puzzled expression on her face.

"Yes, three of us have."

"Who?"

"Mother, Becky and Allan went on vacation to Brazil and took a guided tour on the Amazon River. I remember them telling me about it. They loved it and said it was the most unusual trip they'd ever been on. Allan seemed especially fascinated with the wildlife and the exotic plants they saw."

"How about Becky, did she make any specific comments?" Latimer asked.

"No, she just said she wished she could have talked to the locals more."

"Do you remember where they went exactly?"

"I knew they flew to Peru and then went on a big river boat and all that."

"When was this?" Latimer asked.

"At least a year or so ago, I don't remember exactly."

"Did your father go as well?"

"No, he couldn't get away, as usual." She looked at Latimer with a strange look. "That's where they got the poison, didn't they?"

"I'm afraid so. I got the report back from the Anscott Research, it came from there. At least now we know it was either Allan or Becky," he said, still stroking his beard. "Which one is anybody's guess."

"No wonder Mother got so upset. She must be frantic. Her precious little boy could be a murderer. That would be something." She looked at Latimer with a cynical smile. "I can just imagine what would happen to him in prison. He wouldn't last a day."

"How about Becky?" Latimer asked. "Do you think she could be the one?"

"I don't know. I suppose so, but my bet is on Allan. He really hated Father and I can't say that my father loved his son all that much either." She got up. "I have some tea, would you like some?"

"That would be nice, thanks." Latimer was sure it would be some of her health teas and would definitely taste terrible.

When she came back she carried two mugs and handed him one. "You will be surprised how good it is."

He tried it.

"It is good," he said and took another sip. "What is it?"

"It's called Linden Blossom tea with lemon spice and comes from Germany."

"It's delicious. Maybe I can take some home to let Glenda try it?" He was really surprised.

"Sure, I'll let you have a box for free and then if she likes it, you can buy it from me." She sounded pleased. "Is there anything else you want to know? My next appointment is in a few minutes." She stood up.

"I think this will do. As usual, you've been most helpful." Latimer walked toward the door and shook her hand. "Thanks for your information, Sylvia."

It took Latimer thirty minutes to reach Mr. Burger. He was a few minutes late and hoped Margit Lowell was still there. He looked around the restaurant, until he saw her way in the back at one of the small, round tables with a coke in front of her. She looked at him with fear in her eyes.

"I almost left. I thought you weren't coming," she said.

"Can I get you something to eat, Margit?" he asked as he stood at the table.

"I'll have what you have, Sir."

Latimer went to the counter and ordered two Burger meals. He looked back at where the girl sat. She was short, petite, with dark, brown hair held back in her neck with a rubber band. Her face was heart-shaped with a tiny nose and dark, brown eyes. She was still dressed in her gray uniform, designed especially for kitchen personnel.

"Here we are," Latimer said as he placed the two meals on the table. "I hope you're hungry. I got you a double burger and French fries." He smiled at her reassuringly as he sat down. "I won't tell my wife I'm eating this. She wants me to lose weight. As you can see, she's right," he said as he pointed to his middle.

She smiled a thin little smile.

"You look ok to me."

"Now, what is it you want to tell me, Margit, that has you scared about the Hellman house?" he asked as he bit into his hamburger.

"I don't get into the family room of the house much since I work in the kitchen," she said, haltingly. "There are times when everybody is busy and then they have me clear the table or something like that. With Mr. Henry gone, they were short of help and told me to clear away some dishes in the family room." She had relaxed a little as she went on. "Mr. Grant and Mr. Allan were there. Mrs. Hellman had gone to her room. They were arguing in a loud way so I couldn't miss what they were saying."

"What was it they were arguing about?" Latimer had stopped eating. This was indeed interesting.

"It had to do with some papers that were burned in Mr. Hellman's bedroom. Mr. Grant was yelling at Mr. Allan to make sure all of them were burned, because Mr. Allan wanted to keep some. Mr. Grant told him if he wanted everybody in the family to be safe he, better do as he said or he would take them himself and do it. Then Mr. Allan said that Henry knew about them, but now that he was dead, it didn't matter anymore." Margit's hands were shaking as she took another bite of the hamburger. "I don't know what all that means, but it doesn't sound good, does it, Mr. Latimer?"

"No, it doesn't Margit. Did they say anything else?"

"The last thing I heard was when Mr. Allan yelled at Mr. Grant that he didn't have to take orders from him. He said he had handled everything just fine up till now and didn't need Mr. Grant to interfere in his business. That is when Mr. Grant got really upset and nearly hit him and said he was a stupid, spoiled fool and would be the death of his mother before it was all over." She picked up the last of the French fries and looked up at Latimer. "That's all I heard, because I had to take the dishes back to the kitchen. "I know something terrible happened in that house, Mr. Latimer. I don't like working there and will find another job as soon as I can."

Latimer was on his way back to the office when his cell phone rang. It was Brighton. He had gotten the report back from the lab in New York of the tape.

"I can come by on my way back to my office," he said. "I'm only five minutes away. See you then."

Brighton sat at his desk with a folder in his hand.

"Here's the report on the tape we sent off. They couldn't find out any more than we did and agreed the perp could be a woman or a slightly built man. There were no facial features on the tape for the computer to enhance. The whole thing was a flop," Brighton said.

Latimer told him what he found out from Sylvia and Margit.

"That narrows it down to Allan, Becky and Grant, doesn't it? I don't think it's enough for a warrant. Besides, we can't arrest all three of them." Brighton sounded frustrated. "The killer on the tape isn't big enough to be Grant anyway."

"The only way I can interview Patricia is if you go with me," Latimer said. "She won't talk to me anymore. I'm sure she told all the kids to do the same." Latimer suddenly had an idea. "I have an appointment with Allan tomorrow at three. "What if you come with me? He may not say anything, but many times his reaction to questions can be just as revealing."

"That sounds great." Brighton reached for the phone and dialed Allen Hellman. The man was reluctant at first, but after Brighton threatened him with bringing him in, he agreed. It was the same with Becky. She was drunk again when she answered the phone. Brighton told her they would be at her place tomorrow at two.

"Why so late?" Latimer asked.

"This way she will be drunk and likely to be more uninhibited with her responses," he said. He walked around the desk toward the door. "It's time to go home. I will see you tomorrow at two. If you want to ride with me, meet me in the parking lot at one-thirty."

It was two the next day when Latimer and Brighton drove up at Becky's condo. She opened the door herself this time. She wore a loose fitting robe and had a wine glass in her hand.

"Come on in. Sorry I'm not dressed, but that's the way it is." She slurred her words.

Latimer and Brighton took a seat on the couch, while Becky sat opposite in a chair.

"What do you want to know?" she said in an angry tone.

"If you don't want to get arrested again, you better act in a civilized way, Ma'am," Brighton said before he asked her anything. This time you won't get off so easy."

"I'll be good, I promise," she said with a lopsided smile.

"Tell us about your trip to the Amazon, Becky," Latimer said.

"Mom told me not to talk to you, Mr. Latimer," she said like a pouting child.

"Do you always do what your mom tells you?" he answered with a twinkle in his eyes.

"What do you want to know about it? It was just a dumb trip down some horribly stinky river with lots of heat and rain on the way. I hated it. It was Allan who loved it."

"Did you stop in any of the villages along the way?" Latimer asked.

"We did. I didn't want to go, but Mom made me. She said I might learn something about how the rest of the world lives." She made a movement of disgust. "If I had to spend another day in that place, I would've killed myself."

"Talking about killing, did you see Allan buy anything from anyone during your trip?" Brighton asked.

"I did see him with an old man who sold handmade trinkets. It was junk, I don't know why he wanted it. In the end he didn't buy anything."

"Did you buy anything, Becky?"

"I did. I got to talk with a real medicine man in one village. I didn't stay long, but my mom and Allan were very interested in his healing potions. He was convinced they were better than what the white doctors used. They talked to him during most of the time we stopped there, until they had to return to the boat to continue the trip." She took another sip of wine.

"Did either of them buy something from the man?" Latimer asked.

"I don't know. I had gotten bored and left to go back to the boat. That sort of thing was not for me. The bugs and the heat had gotten to me."

"Did you see Allan or your mother come back with a souvenir?"

"No, they said they didn't find anything they liked."

"Did the boat stop at any other village?" Brighton asked.

"Oh yes, we stopped at several more. I didn't bother getting off the boat after the first one. They looked all the same to me."

"How about your mom and Allan, did they get off each time?" Latimer asked.

"Yes, they did. Both of them found some things in several places to bring back as gifts. I have no idea what they were and I don't care." She sipped her wine again. "They never showed me anything they bought."

Latimer took a good look at her. She was clearly drunk. Not to the point of last time, but getting there fast. He tried to decide whether she was a good actress or told the truth. It was hard to tell. There was no fear in her eyes, no hesitancy he could detect in answering their questions. Although, he knew, most murderers have to be convincing liars if they want to get away with it.

"Why do you think your mom didn't want you to talk to us, Becky?" he asked her.

"I don't know. It's probably because she thinks her precious boy Allan did something wrong down there and she doesn't want him to get in trouble."

"What do you think he could have done?" Latimer asked, careful not to get her mad.

"Maybe she thinks he bought some poison or something like that. I wouldn't put it past the little weasel." She took another sip.

"You don't like Allan very much, do you, Becky?" Latimer said.

"I just wish Mom would let him grow up." There was a hint of disgust in her voice.

"That is all we wanted to know, Becky. Thanks for being so honest with us." Latimer got up. "Don't bother getting up, we'll let ourselves out."

"Do you think she was telling the truth, Latimer?" Brighton asked on the way down in the elevator.

"I think she was, but with these people, there's no telling. Let's go, we will be just in time to talk to Allan."

Chapter 15

It was a little after three when they drove up at the Hellman estate. The maid let them in. Allan was in the family room by himself. Patricia was nowhere to be seen. He seemed nervous and ill at ease.

"We have some questions we want to ask you, Mr. Hellman," Brighton said.

"My mother told me I don't have to talk to you." He sounded petulant.

"You do, Allan. I'm with the police and this is a murder investigation. If you refuse, I will take you in for questioning. I don't think you want me to do that, do you?" Brighton had a hard time hiding his dislike.

"I will not talk to Mr. Latimer. He's not with the police." Allan looked at Latimer with defiance.

"I would not be so sure about that if you want to inherit the fifty million," Latimer said. "I'm still on the case and the rules of the Will are in place."

"Now that we have that cleared up, let's get on with the questioning," Brighton said and cleared his throat. "Have you ever been to the Amazon River, Allan?"

The young man looked at Brighton with a moment of indecision.

"I did go last year with my mother and Becky," he finally said. "We took a tour on the river on a big boat.

"Did you stop at some villages on the way?" Latimer asked.

"Yes, we did."

"What did you buy?"

"Nothing. We bought absolutely nothing." He sounded adamant.

"Your sister Becky tells us you bought some souvenirs." Latimer said. "What were they?"

"I don't remember. It was mostly worthless junk."

"Becky also said you talked to a medicine man at the first stop. Did you buy something from him?" Latimer leaned forward and watched him closely.

Allan moved uneasy in his chair and looked down at his hands.

"I don't remember, it was a long time ago." His voice sounded weak.

"It hasn't been that long ago, Allan," Brighton said. "Did you buy some medicine from him and kill your father and Henry with it?"

Allan looked at him with fear and anger at the same time.

"You are crazy. I didn't buy poison if that's what you mean. You can't come here and accuse me of killing my father." His voice took on a high pitch. "I won't stand for this kind of treatment. I will tell my mother and my lawyer. She will see to it you two lose your lousy little jobs." He was shouting at both of them.

"Remember Allan, it's my job to get you your money. If you want me to give up on it and declare it a dead case, you're going to have to wait ten years to get rich. You better think twice before you lose your temper with me. It didn't work with Becky either." Latimer talked in a calm voice and looked him in the eyes with a hard stare. "I'm tired of being insulted by your family. From where I sit, you are a bunch of obnoxiously rude people, who have never learned the most basic good manners of society. You will either talk to me in a polite tone or I will walk out of here and let you wait for your inheritance." Latimer was really putting on the anger.

Allen shrunk into the couch as if he had been whipped.

"I didn't mean to be rude. I just don't want to go to jail for something I didn't do," he said in a pitiful tone. "I didn't kill my dad. I know I didn't like him, but I didn't kill him."

"Did Becky buy something in one of the villages?" Latimer asked in a more gently tone.

"She got off the boat at every stop and walked around like the rest of us. She said she wanted to talk to the people and find out how they lived and such." He had recovered some of his composure. "We actually had to wait on her one time, before the boat could go on, because she was still talking with some village people."

"She told us she only left the boat at the first stop," Brighton said. "You are telling us she got off every time and bought a lot of things?"

"She was the first one off and the last one back on at every stop. She was lying to you if she said that." He sounded sure of himself now. "I remember, because I got tired of the bugs and the humidity. I didn't enjoy myself one bit on that trip. Mother and Becky were exploring and talking to people at every stop."

"Do you think Becky could have bought some poison from one of the medicine men?" Latimer asked.

"I wouldn't put it past her. She's a disgusting drunk and hated my father," he said with malice. "Maybe she needs to go to prison for what she did."

Both Latimer and Brighton were glad to get out of there.

"This is the most dysfunctional family I've met in a long time," Latimer said. "They are literally tearing each other up, just to get at that money."

"I have a feeling Patricia knows which one of her children killed her husband," Brighton said, "but she will never tell."

"I agree. Both Becky and Allan lied and accused each other. I wish we could put them both behind bars just for general principles," Latimer said. "Unfortunately, that is not going to happen. Instead, we have to find a way to figure out which one of these two miserable sots gets to inherit fifty million dollars and which goes away for good."

"I wish I knew how to figure that one out, Latimer," Brighton said with a deep sigh.

"That makes two of us," Latimer agreed. "Something will come up and we'll find out. It always does." He smiled at Brighton. "Hang in there, Kid. We'll do it together, just like last time." They drove up to the precinct. Latimer got out of the car and waved. "I'll see you later."

His cell phone rang as he drove off. It was Glenda.

"Hi, honey, I went home early today."

"Are you not feeling well?" Latimer asked with concern.

"No, I'm fine. I've put in so many hours lately, Cassie said for me to go home and rest. She left as well. She and Jerry are taking a trip to Washington to visit one of the facilities. She wants him to go with her."

"Maybe I can come home and we'll relax together?" He chuckled. "Seriously, I'm done for the day and was going to go home anyway. Can I go by the store and get something good for dinner? We haven't had steak for a long time."

"That sounds great. Make sure you bring everything to go with it," she said.

When Latimer walked in the door, his cell phone rang. He put the bag of groceries on the kitchen counter and gave Glenda a fleeting kiss while he answered it.

"Latimer, this is Andrea Bellami."

"How good to hear from you Andrea, how are you doing?" He asked.

"I'm fine. The reason I call, I was at a meeting yesterday and talked to Linda Hellman. She is Dr. Hellman's wife. She told me something you might be interested in."

"What is that?"

"Linda was at a family meeting the other day at the Hellman's house with her mother-in-law Patricia. They were discussing the Will, of course. Patricia told the children not to talk to you if at all possible, and lie if they had to. Then she said, there was something in Henry's room that would prove who the killer was, and she couldn't let that happen. She said she had been over it with a fine tooth comb, but hadn't been able to find whatever it was. Allan promised he would look and make sure it would never be found." Andrea took a deep breath. "I just thought you aught to know about this."

"Thanks, Andrea. I think I'll give Det. Sgt. Brighton a call and maybe we can get a search warrant for Henry's and Mr. Hellman's rooms. I appreciate you letting me know about this. Did she say anything else of interest? Maybe I should go and interview her tomorrow." He sounded excited.

"That might be best since I don't remember everything she said," Andrea said.

"By the way, how is the baby?" Latimer asked.

"He is well. Little Peter is growing like a weed. He is a joy and Peter bought him a football the other day. I'm afraid it'll be a while for him to be a quarterback." She laughed. "We were saying the other day, we still can't get over it that Jerry Sanders is now richer than all of us put together. Peter says, at work he's taking it all in stride and is still the same sloppy, lovable guy who is always late for everything. That reminds me, we're going to have a birthday party for Peter in three weeks. It'll be on February 28th at our house. That's a weekend. You and

Glenda are definitely invited. You'll get an invitation in the mail. I hope you can come."

"That sounds wonderful. Maybe by that time this case will be solved," he said. "I'll let Glenda know. Give my regards to Peter."

As soon as he hung up, he called Brighton and told him what Andrea had said.

"I hope this is enough for a search warrant," Brighton said. "I will ask the Chief right away and let you know when and if we're going out there. I really need a break in this case. The Chief is on my back as usual. I don't know how many times a judge will let us search those two rooms," he added.

"Let me know. I'm off the rest of this afternoon. Glenda and I are having dinner at home," he said. "I'll talk to you in the morning."

Latimer walked in the kitchen after he hung up. Glenda had started fixing dinner.

"We're invited to Peter Bellami's birthday party," he said. "It's on February 28th."

"Was that Andrea Bellami?" Glenda asked.

"It was. You heard me tell Brighton what she told me. I hope he gets that search warrant tomorrow. I think I'll go with him. It'll be quite a scene with Patricia, I imagine. She has gotten quite unfriendly these days. I think she's scared one of her children is going to be in trouble." Latimer watched Glenda cut up the salad material. "Do you want me to do some of that?"

"That's alright, honey, I can manage. Just get us something to drink and start the fireplace. We can eat in the living room. It'll be cozy."

It turned out to be a nice evening. They talked about the case and Glenda shared about her work.

"Cassie and Jerry are doing well, I think," Glenda said. "He has adjusted to his role and she has learned to allow him to be himself. Since the party, she understands it works better than forcing him to become a part of the company hierarchy. He is and will always be Jerry Sanders, the happy computer guy, working at Bellami Trucking. There is no doubt he loves his Cassie and she's crazy about him."

"We need to have them, as well as Emily and Richard, over for dinner soon. I miss them all. What do you think?" Latimer asked Glenda.

"That sounds wonderful. I will ask Cassie when they get back from their trip," Glenda said. "They should be home by Saturday, unless they make a mini vacation out of it."

The fireplace gave the room a wonderful, warm, cozy feeling as they sat, enjoying each other into the late evening.

The next morning greeted Latimer with a white snow cover when he walked to his car. It wasn't deep, but the driving would be treacherous until the snow plows had cleared the roads. It took him twice as long as usual to get to his office. Sue Ellen was not there when he arrived. He put on a pot of coffee and picked up the newspaper by the front door. It was cold and dreary outside.

"I declare, Latimer darlin', you are here before me. That hasn't happen in a long time. I must be slippin'. Sue Ellen sounded upbeat.

"Let me guess, you had a date with Wayne last night," Latimer said.

"I did. He's asked me to marry him." She stood in front of Latimer and held out her engagement ring. It had the tiniest diamond on it he had ever seen. "Ain't it pretty?" She looked at it from all sides. "I was so surprised."

"Congratulations, Sue Ellen. I wish you two the best. When do I get to meet your fiancé?" Latimer asked after he gave her a big hug.

"I don't know. He works all day, but I'll invite you to our wedding, that's for sure." She was beaming. "I can't believe I'm an engaged woman."

"What's his last name?"

"His full name is Wayne Edward Morris. That means I'm going to be Mrs. Sue Ellen Morris, imagine that." She swirled around in her chair. "That reminds me, Latimer darlin', the new furniture you had me order online is coming today, remember?"

"I had you order it, or you wanted to order it?" he asked with a twinkle in his eyes. "We can count it as your wedding present, how's that?" He was laughing. "I probably won't be able to afford to buy you one, after I pay for all that stuff you bought."

"Oh, come on now. It ain't that bad, you'll see." She was excited as she poured his cup of coffee. "Here, let's celebrate. This is a good day all the way around."

Latimer's phone rang. It was Brighton.

"The Chief is getting a search warrant, Latimer. I'm waiting for it to get here. I'll pick you up at your office before I head out there as soon as I have it." Brighton sounded excited. "I sure hope we find something we can use, because the Chief says he won't ever get another one."

It was two hours later when they drove up to the Hellman estate. Four officers came with Brighton to conduct the search. They drove in a separate car and stood ready to knock down the door, when it seemed nobody would answer. Brighton rang the bell several more times until the maid finally opened it.

"Mrs. Hellman doesn't want to see you," she said in a frightened voice. "I'm not allowed to let you in."

"We have a search warrant, Miss, you don't have a choice," Brighton said and waved to the men to enter. The maid stepped aside with a frightened look. "I'm going to be in trouble." No one listened to her.

Latimer walked in after Brighton and showed the men where the bedrooms were. Patricia and Allan Hellman came into the hallway from the family room.

"What do you think you're doing?" Allan was screaming in his high pitch voice. "Mom, do something, they're breaking into our house!"

Brighton held up the warrant to Patricia and said, "We have a warrant to search Henry Gossomer's room and your husband's bedroom, Mrs. Hellman. Please step aside and let my men through. We can do this nice or we can break down the doors if that's what you want. The choice is yours." His voice was calm.

"I want that man out of my house," Patricia said, pointing to Latimer.

"He stays." Brighton looked at her with an icy stare. She didn't say anything more and walked back into the family room, followed by Allan. He was shouting threats to call the lawyer the whole way.

Latimer and Brighton went up to Henry's room and watched the men take it apart inch by inch. They even knocked on the walls to hear for any sign of a door or a hidden compartment. On Latimer's suggestion, they picked up the corners of the carpet. Yet after two hours of searching, they found nothing. Latimer could feel the frustration build in the room. Whatever it was Henry had hidden, it had to be here. When the men continued on to Mr. Hellman's room, he stayed and walked slowly through the room and then stood, thinking. If it was him, where would he have hidden evidence so that no one could find it? Slowly, ever so slowly his eyes took in every possible inch of the room.

Suddenly, he remembered Henry's last words. 'My bed…look.' Latimer walked over to the big bed. It had four short, heavy posters, each with a big, round knob on top. He let his hand glide over each and found a rough spot on the right side of the headboard. He tried to turn it. Nothing happened. Then he pulled it and jiggled it upwards. It was moving! He called one of the officers.

"Harry, I think this is what we're looking for. Just pull on it."

"Yes, Sir." The man was still wearing his gloves. The knob was difficult to pull up, until Harry used both hands. Once it was all the way out, he looked inside and saw a small bottle containing a tiny amount of whitish liquid. Gently, he lifted it out and put it inside a plastic bag.

"Please, be careful Harry, that's highly toxic poison," Latimer said. "It will be very interesting to find out who's finger prints we'll find on there."

"We hit the jackpot," Brighton said, beaming. "How about trying the other knobs? Maybe there is more where that came from."

They did, but none of them came loose.

In spite of turning Mr. Hellman's bedroom upside down, they found nothing there.

Patricia and Allan Hellman watched in silence as the police finally left the house.

Chapter 16

When Latimer returned to his office, a large truck stood outside the front door. Two men were carrying in furniture. He was astonished to see his office was empty. Sue Ellen stood, with a big smile, directing the men with her booming voice.

"That goes in the other office." She waved her hand as the men carried a dark, wooden desk into his office. It had a matching chair to go with it as well as two chairs in the front. Latimer looked for the wilting palm tree in the corner. It was gone. So was his bookshelf. It had been replaced by one which matched his desk. He stood in total shock.

"Sue Ellen, what happened to getting a new filing cabinet and a desk for you?"

"Latimer darlin', I couldn't buy me something nice and let you make due with the old stuff. Now we'll look like the most successful detective agency in town." She was pleased with her purchases. "I'm plum excited, aren't you?"

He looked at her, not knowing whether to laugh or be angry. Instead, he turned around and drove to the precinct. Maybe Brighton had some results on the fingerprints by now. He didn't want to say anything to Sue Ellen while he was angry.

Brighton was in his office. He had heard from the fingerprint lab. They found Henry's prints on there and several others. So far they had not found a match in the database.

"None of the family members would have prints on file," Latimer said, "except Becky. We have to get them somehow. I'm certain they will never give them to us voluntarily. My name seems to be on the black list with Patricia." He stroked his beard. "You know what, Grant told me several times he would do anything to help me find the killer. Let's see if he means it. It would be very simple to bring us a drinking glass from Allan and Patricia the next time he goes over to visit. With

Sylvia, we simply ask and she will probably cooperate without a problem."

"That would be great. Otherwise, we'll never get them," Brighton said. "The poison is being sent to the Anscott Research Laboratories tomorrow. I'm sure they will love to get their hands on it for research."

Latimer dialed Grant's number and explained to him that he needed fingerprints from all of them.

"I will try my best. We're having a family powwow tomorrow evening at Mom's. Everyone has been ordered to show up," Grant said. "Do you have any idea what this is all about?"

"I sure do, but I'm going to let your mother tell you the details. The police got a search warrant and found the poison in Henry's room. We need to compare the fingerprints on the bottle," Latimer explained to him.

"How am I going to do that?" Grant asked. "How would I keep them apart?"

"Take a heavy pen and watch until one person puts down an empty plastic cup and put their name on it and stash it somewhere," Latimer said.

"We don't use plastic cups at my mom's house. She hates them."

"You're a smart guy, think of something."

"I will try, Latimer. I'll bring the stuff to your office the next day." He sounded hesitant. There was a big silence on the line. "Suddenly, I feel like a snitch."

"You want to solve the murder of your father and Henry, don't you Grant? This would really help us find the killer." Latimer said.

"This is my family we're talking about. I don't know if I can be responsible for putting one of them in prison for life." He sounded upset.

"I can understand how you feel. However, remember, whoever that person is, they killed two people. It would not be right to let them get away with it." Latimer tried his best to sound convincing.

"I'm sorry, Latimer. I changed my mind, I can't do it. I'm sure you can find another way." He sounded increasingly agitated.

"I have one more question for you, Grant," Latimer said in a calm tone. "It has come to my attention that Allan burned some papers in your father's fireplace in the bedroom. Do you know anything about that?"

There was a sudden silence on the line.

"I have no idea what you're talking about, Latimer," he finally said. "As a matter of fact, I don't want to talk to you anymore. Mom is constantly upset with your accusations into this matter. This whole mess is tearing our family apart and I won't be a part of it. Please, don't call me again. I'm getting to the point I don't care about the money. It isn't worth it to see my mother in such a state of turmoil, because you are snooping around in our lives." He was strangely calm.

"Let me know if you change your mind, Grant." Latimer was frustrated when he hung up.

He told Brighton what Grant had said.

"This puts Grant right back on top of the suspect list. That much for changing and wanting to help," he added.

"Maybe we can go over to Sylvia's apartment again and see if we can't get her fingerprints without her knowing it." Brighton said.

"You would get yourself in real trouble doing that, Det. Sgt." Latimer said.

"You could do it, Latimer. You're no longer with the Crime Unit. You could go to any of them and try to take something we can use." Brighton sounded hopeful. "I really think Sylvia will give them to me without all that clandestine stuff. As for the rest, there has to be a way." He stroked his beard. "I don't for the life of me know why Patricia Hellman is so mad at me. I haven't done anything to her that would account for her aggressive behavior."

"She's like a mama bear defending her cubs. There is nothing she can do about me, but she doesn't have to go along with you," Brighton said. "I think she really hates her husband for making a crazy Will like he did. That whole family is pretty strange, if you ask me."

Latimer got up.

"I'm going back to my office. Maybe Sue Ellen is through rearranging the place by now." He nodded at Brighton. "There is nothing more here I can do. Goodbye, Kid."

The truck was gone when he drove into the parking lot. He was almost afraid what he would find.

Sue Ellen sat behind a brand new, shiny desk with a matching chair. A new filing cabinet stood in the corner right next to a new wall unit. Two matching chairs were arranged in front of her desk.

"I see you are finished with your decorating," he said, trying hard not to show he really liked what she had done.

"Admit it, Latimer darlin', you like it." Sue Ellen was all smiles. "I love the place. I feel like a real secretary now."

"And I feel real poor," he said as he walked on into his office. He had to admit it looked very nice with a real live, potted Florida feather palm in the corner. It reminded him of his honeymoon in West Palm Beach. The new desk and matching chairs, together with a wooden book shelf and a large file cabinet presented a professional looking office.

"You like it, right?" Sue Ellen walked in behind him. "I even got you your Florida palm tree. I will water it for you, I promise."

"I like it, but you should have asked me before you bought all this." He waved his hand in a wide gesture. "This must have cost a fortune, Sue Ellen."

"When you solve the case, you won't feel it, darlin'. She sounded cheerful.

"What if I don't?"

"Of course you will, Latimer. You're the smartest detective in the city. Everybody knows that."

He sat down in his new chair behind his new desk and sighed deeply.

"I hope you're right, Sue Ellen. Right now, it doesn't look like it's going to happen any time soon." He looked at her with a solemn expression. "I will have to fire you, because I don't have the money to pay for all this and your salary, too."

Sue Ellen's face fell as she looked at him in shock.

"I'm fired?"

"It looks that way. Make sure you return all this and get my old stuff back." There was the tiniest little twinkle in his eyes.

"You had me there, Latimer darlin'. This time you really had me." She slumped into the chair in front of his desk and took in a deep breath. Latimer was laughing by now.

"I sure did get you, didn't I? I can't stay mad at you, because you got me with that palm tree. It does look a lot prettier than that plastic piece of junk I had before."

"How about the rest of it, you like it, too?" Her face was one big question mark.

"I like it, just don't do it again."

"I promise I won't." Her smile had returned.

"Now that you're a real secretary, how about getting me Sylvia Hellman on the line?" He said. I need to talk to her."

"Hi Latimer, how nice to hear from you," Sylvia said in a cheerful voice.

"I have a favor to ask of you. I need the fingerprints of the members of your family." He tried to sound casual. "Yours included."

"What do you need them for?"

He explained what happened.

"Do you realize you're asking me to be a part of turning in one of my siblings" Her voice had a sudden harshness to it. "I don't think I can do that, I'm sorry."

"Can I have yours?" He held his breath.

"There is no reason for me to give you mine. I didn't do anything wrong and have no intention to be included in the police database for the rest of my life."

"I understand," Latimer said. "I just thought you wouldn't mind. Have a nice day." He felt like he was hitting a stone wall of silence. The family had started to put up a united front. Patricia must've gotten a hold of them after yesterday's search. In a way he could understand, but it made things more difficult for him. He stroked his beard. What else could he do to get those darn fingerprints? Grant and Sylvia had been his first choice to ask. Since they wouldn't do it, the others definitely had no intention to help him.

He suddenly had an idea and called Andrea Bellami.

"Hi, Andrea, it's Latimer. I have a favor to ask."

"Ask away, anything to get away from diapers, feedings and sleepless nights seems wonderful these days." Her voice sounded tired.

"Will you by any chance have another meeting where you see Patricia Hellman again any time soon?"

"I've been invited to her house for a coffee in two days, but I wasn't going to go. It's one of her charities I really don't want to get involved in." There was reluctance in her voice. "Why do you want to know?"

"I need fingerprints from as many of the Hellman family as I can get, except Becky. We have hers. If you go to their house, it would be easy for you to slip something with fingerprints on it in your purse." Latimer stopped talking before he could make it sound too difficult.

"Detective Latimer, you want me to spy for you?" She was laughing. "That sounds exciting and exactly the thing that would interrupt my motherly duties at the moment."

"You would do it?" He sounded surprised.

"Yes, I would. Just think, I might be a part of solving a big crime. Life has been dull lately and I don't get to go or do much these days. This sounds great. I'll have to think about this and come up with a strategy." She was really getting into it. "How would I label the samples, Latimer?"

"Take along some small plastic bags, put a name on it and when you see an item with anyone's print on it, try to snatch it and put it in the appropriate bag. It's that simple."

"I better take a big purse, shouldn't I?"

She sounded like a kid.

"I need to figure out what would be best for me to take without anyone noticing."

"I'm sure you will, Ms. Sleuth," Latimer said, laughing. "Do you want your pay by the hour or the job?"

"Just wait till I tell Peter. He'll be so proud of me for helping you solve a crime."

"Are you sure he won't mind?" Latimer thought he'd better ask.

"Of course not, I decide what I do and don't want to do. This is the 21st century, you know."

"Are you saying I'm somewhat old fashioned in that area?" He was laughing. "All I know, as a married man, I do what my wife tells me to."

"I can't quite believe that, Latimer. You and Glenda have a wonderful marriage. Us younger folks can take notice and learn from you guys."

"Thanks for doing this for me, Andrea. I owe you big time. Give my regards to Peter."

He smiled after he hung up. Her enthusiasm was refreshing.

Latimer and Sue Ellen spent some time arranging his things with the new furniture. He ordered Chinese for both of them.

"You are good to me, Latimer, darlin'," Sue Ellen said in her most lilting Georgia drawl, while munching on her food.

"Try not to butter me up. You're still in trouble about spending all my hard earned money, young lady." He tried hard to sound tough.

His cell phone rang. It was Becky Hellman.

"Latimer, I need to talk to you." She sounded calm, yet somehow Latimer knew something terrible was wrong. "Please come over right away." The phone went dead.

It took twenty minutes to get to her apartment. The maid answered the door. She looked frightened.

"Please, come in, Mr. Latimer. Ms. Hellman isn't doing well." She led Latimer into the living room.

Becky was sitting in her usual place on the couch. Her eyes stared straight ahead. Without looking at him she said,

"I can't go on like this."

"What's the matter, Becky?" Latimer asked and sat next to her. Her forehead was wet with perspiration and her breathing came in shallow gasps. "Did you take an overdose of some medicine, Becky?" He asked. He felt her hands. They were clammy and cold.

"I can't go on like this."

"Why can't you go on like this, honey? You called me, remember? I'm here." He took her hand and held it. "What did you do, Becky?"

"I killed him, Mr. Latimer. I killed my dad." She started to cry.

"Do you want to tell me about it, Becky?" Latimer said softly.

She looked at him with a most pitiful, sad expression.

"Do you have any idea how it feels to have murdered your own father?" She had stopped crying. "He loved me more than all the others. Look how I repaid him. You heard the video. He wants me to straighten out my life and become a lawyer. What a joke. I'm nothing but a drunken slut. He was too nice to say it, but that is what he meant." She had calmed down.

Latimer sat in silence.

"When I heard the video, I knew what I had done. He looked straight at me when he said that one of his children killed him. He knew it was me." She began to tear up again. "There was something about that video that won't leave me alone. It's like he's still here, talking to me."

"Why do you say you killed him, Becky?" Latimer asked gently. "Did you poison him?"

"No. I could've stopped it and I didn't." She looked at Latimer with profound sadness. "I scoffed at him when he told me about turning my life around by trusting God. I laughed at him when he shared with me how Jesus changed his life. I thought he was a foolish old man." She looked at Latimer. "I was the foolish one, because I didn't listen. Now it's too late. He's dead and it's my fault."

"How is it your fault, honey, tell me."

"Remember, I told you we went to the Amazon? Mother and Allan went shopping in that first village and I tagged behind them. I was not the least bit interested in what they bought and just wandered around. After a while, Allan came up to me and handed me a small package. He asked me to keep it for him and put it in my suitcase on the way home. He also told me not to tell anyone about it, not even Mom. He just looked at me and grinned.

"Just do it, Sis," he said, "and don't ask any questions. If anyone asks you about it, tell them you have no idea what's in it." Becky turned to Latimer. "I did as he asked. Now I know it was the poison. I carried it home and when I unpacked my suitcase it was gone. Someone had taken it. I thought it happened at the airport. You know, when they open your suitcase and take stuff they don't want you to bring into the country? I found one of those slips of paper that show it was searched."

"Did you ever ask Allan about it?" Latimer asked.

"No, I put it out of my mind and started drinking to kill the memory, but it won't let me go. When I heard my father talk about one of his kids killed him, I knew it had to be Allan. If I had refused to bring the poison with me, he could not have done it. That's why I say I killed my dad." She was crying again. "I can't deal with it any more and I can't stop drinking." She took the glass on the coffee table and took a sip. It's the only thing that dulls the pain and guilt." She stared straight ahead. "I wish I had told him I loved him when he was so sick. I should have asked him to forgive me for my childish and immature behavior. He would've paid for me to go and finish law school. Instead, I wasted my time with a bunch of losers." She turned to Latimer. "What can I do to make it up to him?"

"You can ask his forgiveness, Becky. I know he's dead. You did not kill him. You had no idea what was in that package Allan asked you to bring in your suitcase. What you did wrong, you withheld your love and affection from your father, especially when he was dying. Remember what he told you about himself? How he turned his life around from a greedy investor to become a generous, kind man, who gave to many good causes. I know you didn't want to hear about his religion. What he wanted you to know about was not religion, but a relationship with Jesus. He gave his life over to him and so should you. You may have made a lot of mistakes, but so have we all. That is what Christianity is all about. God takes broken people and makes them whole again by accepting His gift of love and forgiveness. It is a gift and can't be earned. It can only be accepted by admitting we can't handle things on our own. He's a big God and has no trouble making sense out of our broken lives."

Becky looked at Latimer with great sadness.

"There is no way God would ever want someone like me. Look what I've done with my life. I'm nothing but a rich whore who thought she could use and control men. That's a joke. They controlled me and when they were done with me, they threw me away. I'm nothing but a piece of junk." She was crying again and reached for the glass. Latimer took her hand before she took it and held it in his.

"That is not where your answer lays, Becky. God is an expert at creating something from nothing. He can take you and turn you into the beautiful young woman He always knew you could be. Will you let Him do that by giving Him your life?"

She nodded her head. "Yes."

They sat for a while and neither of them said a word. Finally, Becky got up, took the glass and walked over to the kitchen sink and poured the wine down the drain.

"I want to be free of this, Latimer. I'm going to check myself into a rehab center. I want to turn my life around like my dad did and become the kind of person he always knew I could be. You say it's not too late. Let's see if you're right." She pulled open a drawer and took out a brochure and called a number. It was a rehab center in Glenridge. When she hung up, she turned to Latimer and said, "Will you take me there?"

"I'll be glad to, Becky."

Chapter 17

Before Latimer drove back to the office, he called Brighton to fill him in on what happened.

"Do you think that's enough to get a warrant, Latimer?" Brighton asked.

"It should be enough to haul him in for questioning. The trouble is, he will lawyer up and get out on bail. It wouldn't accomplish much. The only advantage in bringing him in, is to get his fingerprints. If they match the ones on the bottle, you've got him."

"That clinches it. I'm sure the Chief will go along with it." Brighton sounded upbeat. "I can't wait to bring that weasel in and let him roast in a cell overnight. Since you're the one who figured this out, Latimer, I think you should be there when we bring him in."

"Call me when you get the warrant. I'll meet you at the precinct and ride over with you," Latimer said. He got to his office before Sue Ellen went home and told her what had happened with Becky.

"I declare, that poor woman. She's been through the mill," She said. "I sure hope they'll help her in that place." She was straightening the top of her desk. "I'm glad it's Friday. I'm going to Wayne's folks this weekend. They live up in Rocksburg. His whole family is going to come for supper, just to meet me. Imagine that."

"Make sure you take a dictionary so they can understand what you're saying, Sue Ellen," Latimer said with a chuckle. "Once you start with your folksy Georgia sayings, you're going to lose them."

"I hope they won't laugh at me, Latimer."

"They're going to love you, Sue Ellen, especially your Georgia drawl." He sounded sure.

His cell phone rang.

"We'll be leaving in half an hour. Meet me at the parking lot," Brighton said. He sounded excited. He had just solved his second case.

Latimer wasn't so sure. There were too many unanswered questions. Maybe he would sit in on the interrogation and learn more of the details. He had the feeling Allan wasn't going to make it easy. He would rely on his lawyer to get him out before they could ask him anything important. It wouldn't hurt to scare him real good, though.

The Hellman estate looked deserted when they got there. It was getting dark and the weather was still foul. The temperature was dropping rapidly. The maid opened the door and let them in.

"I'm here to see Allan Hellman," Brighton told her.

"Come with me, please," she said and led them to the family room. Patricia and Allan, as well as Grant and William, were sitting in front of the fireplace. They looked at Latimer and Brighton with surprise.

"What do you want?" Patricia asked in a sharp tone.

Brighton stepped toward Allan and said, "Allan Hellman, you are under arrest for the murders of William Karl Hellman and Henry Gossomer." He read him his Miranda rights while he handcuffed him.

"Mom, don't let them do this to me," Allan whined in his high pitch voice.

Patricia stood there, frozen. She turned as white as a sheet and began to cry. William put his arms around her shoulders and helped her sit down. Grant stood silently as he watched Brighton put on the handcuffs.

"Why are you constantly harassing us, Det. Sgt. Brighton," Dr. Hellman said. "You don't have any proof that my brother did this, do you?"

"We have more than enough to hold him," Brighton said in a calm voice. "You may want to get him a lawyer. He's going to need one." He turned to Allan. "Let's go."

Latimer hadn't said a word.

"Mr. Latimer, what is this all about?" Grant asked. "Surely you didn't have anything to do with this?"

"I did, Grant. It is because of my findings they are arresting him. I'm doing what I was hired to do by your father." Latimer looked at him with confidence. "Rest assured. I will solve this case according to Mr. Hellman's last wishes." He turned around and followed Brighton to the car.

Allen was sobbing like a baby as they helped him into the backseat of the police car. He looked around for his mother, but Patricia was nowhere to be seen. Latimer sat next to Brighton up front.

"At least we'll get his fingerprints. That should clinch the case," Brighton said as they pulled out of the driveway. "There is no way the little weasel would have ever given them to us."

By the time they got to the precinct, Allan's lawyer was waiting for them. Latimer didn't even bother to go in. The lawyer would prevent any useful questioning. He got into his car and went home. He was looking forward to a nice weekend. The case could wait. He vowed, nothing and nobody would get him away from the cozy fireplace for two days until Monday morning.

It was not to be. The call came the next day. Grant Hellman called from the hospital. Patricia was found in the morning near death in her bed. She had tried to commit suicide.

"She's on life support and in a coma. The doctors don't know if she will survive, Latimer. This is your fault. I'm letting you know that no one in this family will talk to you again. We don't care about your assignment from Dad. You are not to set foot or come near our house, do you understand?"

"I'm so very sorry about your mother, Grant. I'm only doing what I was hired to do and I do understand your anger." He was upset about Patricia, too. He knew she did not try to kill herself because of Allan being in jail. There was more to this. She knew something she couldn't deal with anymore and tried to end her life. He realized, this would essentially halt his investigation. On the other hand, the case was not solved, no matter how it looked. Either Allan Hellman did not do this, or he did not do it by himself. Latimer was convinced Patricia knew the whole story. As a mother, she was devastated and couldn't cope losing one or even two of her children to a life in prison.

If she lived, he would go talk to her when no one was around. One phone call from Grant would not stop him. It wasn't his style to give up until the case was solved. He was absolutely convinced there were facts he had not discovered yet. The case would just have to wait till Monday.

Later in the morning, Brighton called with the results from the fingerprint lab. One of the prints belonged to Allan Hellman. It was only a partial print, but enough to identify it as his. Brighton doubted Allan would be allowed to post bail with a possible double murder rap. The hearing was scheduled for Monday morning. Brighton was elated. This would look good with the Chief.

"We do work well together, Latimer. I could've never done it without you," he said. Latimer could almost see his bright smile over the phone.

"Not so fast, hotshot. We're not done yet. There's still much more to figure out in this case. We'll get together on Monday and discuss it. Also, I would like to talk to Allan or at least be there for the interview," Latimer said.

"That can be arranged. I'll let you know after the hearing," Brighton said.

"Now let me enjoy my weekend, Kid. There's nothing more we can do until next week. Go do something fun with Hattie instead." Latimer chuckled and hung up.

It was later in the afternoon Grant called again. He sounded angry.

"I can't believe this, Latimer. My mom wants to talk to you. She woke up an hour ago. She's extremely weak and can barely talk. She insisted I ask that you visit her today."

"I will be there as soon as I can," Latimer said. He groaned as he looked at the cozy fireplace. Glenda was reading a book, sitting in her favorite chair.

"So much for your quiet weekend at home," she said. "I hate for you to go out in this awful weather. Make sure you dress warm and drive careful."

"It will not be pretty out there. I can't refuse. Maybe she's ready to tell me what she knows. This could be the breakthrough I need to solve this case. I will be back as soon as I'm done talking to her." He kissed her before he left.

On his way to the hospital, he wondered what it was Patricia wanted to talk to him about. He didn't think she would incriminate any of her other children. So what could it be?

Everyone, except Becky, was there when he got to the room. They stared at him with icy looks and did not say a word when he greeted them.

"I wonder if you would mind stepping out while I talk to your mother," he said after he made sure Patricia was awake. She looked pale and weak, with several IVs coming out of her arms. She acknowledged him with a nod. Reluctantly, everyone left the room. Latimer closed the door behind them and walked up to her bed.

"Patricia, what is it you want to talk to me about?" he said in a gentle voice.

She looked at him with a strange, forlorn look as if it was too late to change things in her life.

"I don't want to die before I say what I have to say." Tears rolled down her cheeks.

"Patricia, you're not going to die. I'm sure the doctors are doing everything they can to help you," he said reassuringly.

"It won't be enough, because I don't want it to be." There was some of the strength in her voice he knew she had.

"What is it you want to tell me?" He asked.

"I want to ask you to stop investigating my family. We have enough trouble as it is. William is dead. There is no reason to dig up things that will destroy us all. Please." She looked at him with pleading eyes.

"I can't do that, Patricia. I'm bound by my contract to find out who killed your husband. I took the money. It would be dishonest of me to let things go, just because you ask me to."

"I will pay you whatever you ask if you stop. Then you can pay the money back to Gary Norton and everything will be legal." Her breathing was labored as she talked.

"It would still be dishonest, Patricia. What is it you're so afraid I'm going to find?" He leaned forward and took her hand. "What is so terrible you can't live with? Tell me."

"I can't. There are things which would make life more difficult for all of my kids if I told you. It wouldn't change anything, but make matters worse for everyone. I love my children and I will not help destroy their lives." She was crying and started to convulse. Latimer rang for the nurse. By the time she came, Patricia had lost consciousness.

Latimer walked past the Hellman family without a word. They did not try to stop him, but stood together in fear, knowing this could be the end of their mother's life. He had not found out a thing. What Patricia asked him to do confirmed what he had thought all along. She held the key to this case.

On his way home he felt frustrated and at a loss of where to go from here. Hearing her despair, he was afraid Patricia Hellman did not want to go on living. He knew she was a strong woman and could very well decide not to fight to stay alive. What could he have said to make a difference? He didn't have any idea what it was she tried so hard to hide from him and her children. Neither could he think of anything that would have made a difference. He wondered if Allan knew the truth. It would be interesting to be able to question him on Monday. The man didn't have the backbone his mother had. It might be easier to get him to talk.

He felt tired as he turned into his parking spot. Deep in thought, he barely acknowledged the doorman and was glad when he walked into the warmth of his condo. The fire was still going strong and Glenda handed him a cup of hot coffee as he sat down in his favorite chair.

"Did you find out anything new?" Glenda asked.

"Nothing. The woman is ready to die and doesn't want to ruin her children's lives with the secret she's hiding. I have a feeling she knows the whole truth, but would rather die than ruin her children's future. She even offered me money if I would agree to stop digging for more facts in the case." He leaned back with a deep sigh.

"You learned nothing then?" Glenda asked. "The whole trip was a waste?"

"Essentially, yes. She's trying to avoid the truth in exchange for her life. I admire her for the kind of mother she is. I just wish I knew what it is she's hiding." He took a sip of coffee. "My only hope to find anything new is Allan Hellman. I'm going in on Monday and sit in during the interrogation."

"Do you think he knows what she's trying to conceal?" Glenda asked.

"I don't know. We'll have to wait and see. He definitely handled the bottle of poison. No one knows if Patricia's fingerprints are on it. I doubt it. She probably didn't know he bought it when they were down there and then gave it to Becky to carry it out of the country." Latimer got up and stoked the fire. "The little weasel, he didn't even have the guts to do it himself. Instead he put his sister in danger of being arrested at the airport. He is some miserable excuse of a man," Latimer said with disgust.

Glenda came in with a tray, filled with his favorites, cheese and crackers, and a glass of wine to wash it down.

"You spoil me, sweetheart." He kissed her as she reached past him and put the tray on the coffee table.

"That's because I love you, honey. You deserve to be spoiled."

Monday morning was another cold and dreary day. It looked like snow was on the way. Latimer got a call from Brighton. Allan Hellman had a hearing at ten this morning. Brighton would interview him right after. Latimer left home at eleven and went straight to the precinct. He sat behind the one-way glass window as Allan was led into the interrogation room. His lawyer was waiting for him. Brighton walked in with a cup of coffee in hand and sat down opposite Allan and the lawyer. He put down a folder and turned the recording device on.

"Good morning, Gentlemen," Brighton said and flashed his bright smile. "My name is Det. Sgt. Brighton and I'm here to interview you, Mr. Hellman. You have been charged with the murder of William Carl Hellman and Henry Gossomer. You have been denied bail. We have read you your Miranda rights." He looked at the lawyer and raised his eyebrows.

"I'm Matt Lauer, Mr. Hellman's legal advisor. My client is innocent and I demand that he be released immediately. We are outraged he is being held without bail."

Brighton didn't answer and took another sip of his coffee. He looked at Allan. The young man sat slumped in his seat, with a dejected look on his face. His folded hands on the table were trembling visibly and he looked close to tears. Apparently, the lawyer had told him not to say anything, because he sat in silence, with his eyes lowered and his lips in a perpetual pout.

"Mr. Hellman, I want to tell you first of all, we found your fingerprint on the bottle of poison used to kill your father and Henry Gossomer. Can you tell me how that got there?"

Allan looked at Matt Lauer. The man nodded.

"I touched it when Becky bought it while we were at a village on the Amazon River." His voice was thin and halting.

"What was the purpose of you buying it?" Brighton said.

"I didn't buy it, she did." He sounded insolent.

"Then why aren't her fingerprints on it and yours are?"

"I don't know. I didn't buy it." His voice was high and thin. "She's a drunk and doesn't know what she's doing half the time." He leaned back with a sigh. "I don't know why you are not arresting her.

She did it. She killed my father and Henry." His voice was shrill. Matt Lauer put his hand on his arm to stop him from saying anymore.

"What my client is saying, he has no idea how his print got on the bottle. We must therefore assume, Ms. Hellman wiped her prints off."

"Mr. Lauer, you must admit your theory is ridiculous. If she wiped them off when she supposedly bought the poison, it still begs the question how your client's prints got on there since then. Unless he used the poison to murder two people, that is."

The lawyer didn't answer.

"Mr. Hellman, why did you murder your father?" Brighton said without emotion.

"My client didn't murder anyone, Det. Sgt. Brighton. He is an innocent, scared, young man, not used to such harsh treatment as he has been receiving in the last two days." Matt Lauer sounded dramatic. "I protest the harsh conditions in this facility and demand he get better accommodations."

"I'm sorry to say, but we're not the Granger Hotel. If your client doesn't start to cooperate, our jail will be a fond memory when he gets to prison, Mr. Lauer." Brighton sounded tough. "I'm going to ask you again, why did you murder your father? Did you have any one of your siblings help you? If you disclose that kind of information, we might be able to strike a deal. You know how it is. The first one to tell gets the deal, how about it, Allan?"

Allan looked at Lauer with a question on his face. The lawyer shook his head.

"You have only circumstantial evidence and no proof. My client will not say anything, because he is innocent."

Brighton had hit a stone wall. He closed his file and walked out of the room without another word.

Chapter 18

Patricia Hellman hovered on the brink of death for an entire week, before she showed the first signs of improvement. Her doctors declared, while still in critical condition, she would live. Latimer went to see her. She had lost a lot of weight. Her face was gaunt and her eyes without life. She looked like a broken shell of her former self.

"Mr. Latimer, come on in. I have been expecting you." Her voice was weak.

"You have been through a lot, Mrs. Hellman. I came to see if you're up for some questions?" He smiled at her. She seemed at peace and held out her hand to him.

"I guess I gave everyone a scare. I still think it would've been better if I had died. I'm tired of life and want to be with William. He was more of an anchor in my life than I realized." She looked at Latimer with a question in her eyes, "Can you love someone more when they're dead than when they were alive, Latimer?"

"That depends on the circumstances, Patricia. We tend to overlook a person's faults more readily after they are gone, and remember only the good things. It brings us comfort if we loved them and guilt if we didn't. Which one is it for you?" he asked with kindness in his voice. "Your husband was a good man from what I've been able to gather during my investigation."

"You don't think very highly of the rest of us, do you?" There was a sad little smile on her face. "You have seen the ugly side of an outwardly beautiful family." She started to tear up. "Getting this close to dying is a life changing experience. I've had time to look at myself while lying in this bed, watching my children struggle with this situation. The video my husband left for them has profoundly affected all of us, even me. It keeps replaying in my mind and I see William for the first time for the good man he was. The hardest part is that he asked for forgiveness for being a father, trying to teach his children responsibility. All of us, including me, resented him for it." She wiped the tears away with a tissue. "I cannot tell you how sorry I am for not supporting him in that area. Instead, I enabled them to become dependent on his money. What a failure that makes me as a mother." She dabbed at her eyes. "I wish I could undo what I've done, but it is too late for me." She laid her head back and closed her eyes. "I'm going to have to ask you to leave now, Latimer. Suddenly, I'm very tired."

Latimer walked out of the room and ran into Grant Hellman down the hall.

"Grant, how are you holding up?" He asked. "I just came from your mother. She's asleep now. Can we talk?"

Grant looked at him with hesitation.

"I really don't think I want to talk to you, Latimer."

"You really don't want to continue blaming me for your mother's suicide attempt, do you?" Latimer said. "Come with me. Let's go to that small waiting room down the hall and sit for while."

Reluctantly, Grant followed him.

"Grant, I'm sorry about your mother's attempt to kill herself. It looks like she'll be ok. There is something she cannot live with from what she told me."

"Did she say what it was?" Grant asked.

"No, she didn't, but it has to do with protecting some of you kids. I don't think it has anything to do with Allan being in jail. The only thing she said, if I found out about it, it would further destroy your family. Do you have any idea what that could be?" Latimer asked.

"I have no idea. It must be some deep, dark family secret she doesn't want to come out." Grant sighed deeply.

Latimer looked at him with doubt.

"I feel like she knows a lot more than she lets on about your father's and Henry's death. I can only guess. I think she's protecting not just one, but two people who are involved and simply can't live with the idea, two of her children could end up in prison for life."

"Good grief. That would be terrible." Grant looked horrified. "This is some kind of family." He leaned over toward Latimer. "I'm sorry I got so mad at you. It doesn't look like her attempt has much to do with you at all, does it?"

"It has everything to do with protecting her children," Latimer said.

"I went to see Becky," Grant said. "She's going to make it this time. I can feel it. She told me what you did for her. There is something very different about her. The way she tells it, you helped her check herself into rehab. Thanks, Latimer."

"She had reached bottom. I hope it sticks and she goes back to school, the way her father wanted her to." Latimer said.

"That video has had a tremendous effect on all of us," Grant said. "Even William talked about it. It seems it took my father's death to reach us with his message that he loved us and wanted only our best." He looked thoughtful. "I'm looking into becoming a professional investor with a small firm here in Glenridge. With my father's name to help me get in the door, I want to make something of myself." Grant sounded determined. "I've done a lot of soul searching and decided it's time to settle down and see if I can do more than buy cars and chase women. I'm even interested in finding the one and only woman for me." He looked at Latimer with a smile. "Do you have any advice on that front?"

"I wish I had a fool-proof method to find the right one. I've done well twice. I must be doing something right." He smiled. "Both of my wives have made me very happy."

Latimer leaned back in his chair.

"Grant, do you have any idea which one of you, aside from Allan, could have had a hand in killing your father and Henry?"

"Sylvia is the only one left. I definitely would rule out William. He doesn't have any need for my dad's money and is the most stable of all of us. That leaves Sylvia. She's so eaten up with hate for all men I wouldn't put it past her." He frowned. "Although, I've talked to her since then and she seems to have changed as well, and for the better. She told me, the video started her thinking to make something of herself. She actually told me she loved our father." He looked at Latimer with a strange look. "Why don't you think Allan did it by himself? He's not near as dumb as he acts. If that boy wants something, he usually gets it somehow. In other words, he can be pretty determined."

"I don't know why I have a feeling he had help. It's something I've developed over thirty years on the police force. It's not all science and evidence, a good part is called gut feeling." He smiled. "When you get to be my age, experience plays a large part in the equation of solving a crime. And my experience tells me, Allan was not alone in this."

"Don't they say poison is the tool of choice for women?" Grant asked.

"That is what they say. Whether that is true or not, I don't know. Not too many murders are committed that way when looking at the big picture. The main reason could also be, many poisonings are not found out. Look at your father. If he had not left the video, no one would've ever known. I'm sure many old people die from what seems to be natural causes, when all along they've been killed gradually by poison." Latimer got up. "I still wish you would answer the question why you argued with Allan. I do know it had something to do with burning papers in your father's bedroom in the fireplace."

"That's not going to happen. All I can tell you, it has nothing to do with the murder."

"It was nice talking to you, Grant. I've got to go. Take care and I hope your mother will fully recover." Latimer tried hard not to show his frustration.

It was Friday afternoon and it was time to go home. Glenda had invited Jerry, Cassie, Emily and Richard, as well as Peter and Andrea Bellami to dinner at the condo. She had taken the day off. It was the first time they had friends over for a formal dinner since they got married.

Glenda was in the kitchen when he got home.

"You're just in time to help me. The first thing I need you to do is start the fireplace. I had the cleaning woman here this morning. Everything else is ready. We're having shrimp Alfredo, salad and cheesecake for dessert. They should get here by seven." She walked over and kissed him. "Hi, handsome, I'm glad you're home."

"The table looks nice," Latimer said. "I'm looking forward to seeing everybody again. It's been since the company event that I've seen them all." He carried the firewood in from the small balcony, and before long, the wonderful smell of burning wood filled the room.

Peter and Andrea were the first to arrive. They had brought the baby.

"He has grown so much and looks just like you, Peter," Glenda said as she took him in her arms.

"The poor child," Peter said with a big grin, filled with pride.

"Come on in and sit by the fire until everybody gets here," Latimer pointed into the living room.

"You have a beautiful place," Andrea said as she looked around. "It looks perfect for the two of you."

"We are very happy here," Latimer said. "Have a seat. I'll get you some hot tea to warm you up."

The doorbell rang again. It was Cassie and Jerry with Richard and Emily right behind them.

Soon, dinner was ready and everyone sat around the big table. Latimer raised his glass in a toast.

"To good friends," he said with a smile. "Glenda and I are so glad to have you here for the first time. We hope it won't be the last."

"How is your case going?" Andrea asked, once everyone had filled their plates. "I know the charity event at Patricia's was cancelled because she's in the hospital. There are rumors she tried to kill herself. Is that true, Bob?"

"Yes, it is. I think she couldn't live with the fact that two of her children might be guilty of murder. It was touch and go for a whole week, but I think she'll make it."

"That's awful. Do you have any idea who did it?" Peter asked.

"The youngest, Allan, is in jail. I spoke with Brighton today and he says he's having an extremely hard time. I can only imagine how hard, being as spoiled as he is," Latimer added.

"Who is the other?" Cassie asked.

"I don't know. I tried to get Patricia to tell me, but she will never do it. She's determined to protect her children." Latimer said, reaching for another slice of bread. "I'm not even that sure Allan did anything but buy the poison. Unless something breaks, we may never know unless the boy gets so tired of being in jail, he decides to talk."

"From what little I know of him, Allan is the most spoiled, obnoxious man, who never had a chance to grow up. His mother smothered him and never said 'no' to whatever he wanted." Cassie said with disdain in her voice. "That whole family is totally dysfunctional, if you ask me." She turned to her husband. "Jerry and I went to Washington last week. We added on a weekend and toured the city. Jerry had never been there." Cassie sounded happy.

"How are you lovebirds doing?" Latimer asked.

"She is every bit as wonderful as I thought she'd be and I'm even better than that," Jerry said with his boyish grin. "Between the two of us, we are doing great."

"Jerry comes into work every day with this happy grin on his face," Peter said. "People are getting tired of it and swear he pasted it on permanently."

"How can you talk like that, Peter?" Andrea scolded him. "They are in love."

"Just wait till they have a baby and don't get enough sleep to know day from night," Peter added. "I swear the kid sleeps all day, and as soon as we go to bed, he wakes up and cries until we take him into our bed and play. The minute he goes back into his crib, he cries." Peter pretended to be suffering. "There goes the honeymoon."

"We have decided to hold off on children for a while until things have settled down at work for me and Jerry has gotten used to his new life," Cassie said. "Everybody loves him at the company. Ever since that party, he's like a rock star walking in. You'd have thought he gave the greatest speech of the century." She was laughing. "I think he did."

"I've started a new trend among the snobby crowd. Jeans and t-shirts are the preferred dress code for the day." Jerry laughed. "That part is going real well. Everything else, Cassie handles." He sounded happy. "It's going a lot easier than I thought."

"Richard, Emily, how are you two doing? We miss you," Glenda said and looked at the couple with a big smile.

"We are doing well, Mrs. Latimer," Richard said in his formal way.

"Don't you think it's about time you call me Glenda?" She raised her glass toward both of them.

"That sounds wonderful, Glenda," Richard said.

"I miss the two of ye as well. Those were good times when ye stayed with us for a while," Emily said with a warm smile which covered her face with countless tiny wrinkles. Latimer loved her Irish brogue. "Of course, having Jerry with us now has put some excitement into the place. It reminds me when our dear Marten was still with us, God rest his soul. The only difference is, Jerry is a lot messier than Marten, and I thought he was bad. "

Everyone laughed, except Jerry. He shrugged his shoulders and grinned.

"I have to be better at something than that boy was."

Peter asked, "Bob, have you met Grant Hellman? He used to be a friend of mine several years ago. How's he doing? We went to school together. He was wild in those days."

"He's trying to settle down. The murder of his father and butler has rattled him somewhat. He seems to have been closer to his father than the others and said he was a friend to Henry, the butler," Latimer answered.

"I remember him telling me how he hated his old man," Peter said thoughtfully. "He never said anything about the butler. As a matter of fact, I heard him be real rude to the man quite often. It upset me at the time. I met Mr. Hellman and I liked him. He was kind and talked to me about what I wanted to do with my life."

"I think he was sad that his kids didn't do anything but ask for money," Latimer said. "Did he ever say anything to you about that, Peter?"

"Not directly, but he seemed pleased that I wanted to take over my dad's business. He sounded sad and I didn't understand why. I was just a kid then and had no idea that his children were such spoiled brats. Especially Grant. He was wild with drinking, girls and all that kind of stuff. It would be quite a change if he wanted to settle down. I'll believe it when I see it."

"He tried to hit on me several times," Cassie said. "I didn't like him, because he was so full of himself. I know he's good looking, but I don't like that arrogant type. A lot of the girls fell for him and they were sorry after he dumped them." Cassie looked at Latimer. "There were rumors of rape, but I think it was hushed up with money from his mother. I heard, she paid the girls off and his father never knew about it."

"What about later? Did you ever hear anything else that could point to him as being capable of murder?" Latimer asked Cassie and Peter.

"I'm convinced he is very much capable of doing something like that, unless he has really changed," Cassie said.

"I can't see him changing either," Peter said, "unless something drastic has happened. His father's death might have done it. He must be close to forty. I think it's time he does change into a responsible adult."

"I don't think he has to with inheriting fifty million dollars," Cassie said.

"If he killed his father, he gets nothing," Latimer said. "I'm still working hard to find out."

"I remember Henry Gossomer very well," Richard said when there was a lull in the conversation. He was a good man, hard working and devoted to Mr. Hellman. He never said much about the rest of the family, but I knew they didn't treat him very well."

"When did you talk to him last, Richard?" Latimer asked.

"It must have been two weeks before he died, maybe less. We were at a meeting together. We both belong to a butler's club. He mentioned that things weren't well with the family, but said he couldn't talk about it." Richard wiped his mouth with his napkin. "He looked stressed and upset. I was wondering what had happened. He did tell me Mr. Hellman had died. I asked him if he knew what he died of. That's when I noticed Henry had this strange look on his face. He said something I didn't pay any attention to at the time."

"What was it?" Latimer asked.

"Let me see if I can remember. Yes, this is what he said, 'Not all is as it seems. I have to decide what to do about that.' Richard sat deep in thought. "I wish I had pressed him further, but there is a code among professional butlers not to gossip about one's employers. I know Henry took that very seriously."

"If you could guess where he would keep his important papers, where would that be, Richard?" Latimer asked.

"We sat around one day at the meeting and discussed that very point. Since we all live with someone else, there is sometimes a certain lack of privacy. Emily and I don't have that problem, because the Estate is so large. Henry's situation was different. He only had one room and a bath to call his own. I don't think there was much privacy there. He told me he had a bank deposit box and kept all important papers there."

"Did he say what bank?" Latimer tried hard not to sound too excited.

"He didn't say. I do know it was a bank here in Glenridge, because he mentioned he had time to go to the bank during his lunch break."

Latimer leaned back in his chair. This sounded like a break. He would call Brighton and have the Kid get a warrant to open the deposit box as soon as they found out which bank it was. It was a new lead, just what he needed.

Chapter 19

    Brighton received the warrant for the safe deposit box the next afternoon. He called Latimer and together they went to the Glenridge City Bank shortly thereafter. A young man showed them the way to the vault, handed Brighton the key and left. It was located at the bottom of the wall of boxes.
    "I can't wait to see what's in it," Brighton said as he turned the key. The box slid open easily. He put it on the counter in the middle of the narrow room. Latimer took a deep breath as he watched the lid being lifted. The box was empty!
    "Darn," Brighton said, disappointment showing in his voice. "Someone beat us to it and took it out."
    "That's right." Latimer sounded mad. "Somebody did. You're going to have to get a warrant for the security tapes for the last several weeks. It will take forever to go through them since we don't know when the person came and who we're looking for. If the camera doesn't show the number of the box, we'll never find it. Let's ask up front to see who came here. I'm sure they keep a record of all the people who check their boxes. If we are lucky, they'll let us look at it without a warrant. In the meantime, I think you should have this box dusted for fingerprints. Maybe something will come up," Latimer suggested.
    They stopped at the desk outside the volt. It would take quite a while to check the entries over the last three weeks in the large ledger the bank employee handed them. All they could do was check if there was a familiar name. Before they could get past the first page, a middle-aged man in a suit walked up to where they sat.
    "I'm sorry, Gentlemen, I cannot allow you to do this without a warrant. I apologize for the mix-up, but Ms. Miller is new and is not yet aware of our privacy policies in this bank." He took the ledger and closed it. "We will be happy to comply if you'll bring us a warrant."

"That went well," Brighton said as they walked to the car, the safe deposit box in hand.

"We almost got away with it," Latimer said. "I knew the girl was not allowed to give it to us, but it doesn't hurt to try, does it?" He smiled. "You better get that warrant." He turned to Brighton. "I would like to interview Allan Hellman when I get back to the precinct. I know he doesn't have to see me, but I want to try. Maybe he is worn down by his time in jail and is ready to talk to anyone, even me."

"That sounds like a good idea. I can't talk to him without his lawyer present, but you can," Brighton said. "Let's try it." He called the jail and asked the secretary to see if Allan was willing to talk to Latimer.

By the time they drove into the parking lot of the precinct, Brighton was told Latimer would be allowed to talk to the inmate.

"I told you, he is desperate and willing to talk to anyone." Latimer sounded upbeat.

A sad, gaunt and weary looking Allan Hellman walked into the visiting room a few minutes later. He looked at Latimer with a mixture of anger and hope as he sat down opposite from him at a table.

"What do you want?" His voice sounded dull.

"I know you didn't do this, Allan. Or at least you didn't do this alone. There is no reason for you to take the wrap for someone else." Latimer used his most soothing voice and looked at Allan with a convincing expression of sympathy. "If you're innocent, I want to help you, Allan. You don't deserve to be in here for something you didn't do." He was hoping his act was working.

"I know I'm innocent, but nobody here believes me. They say everybody in jail says they're innocent." Allan perked up a little. "Why do you want to help me? You're the one who got me into this place." There was anger in his voice. "It's a nightmare in here." He leaned over and grabbed Latimer's hand. "Please get me out of here. I'll do anything you say." He was nearly in tears.

"That's why I'm here, Allan. I want to help you, but you have to help me first by telling me who poisoned your father and Henry." Latimer asked.

"I don't know. All I did was buy the stuff when we went down to the Amazon. I brought it home and put it in my medicine cabinet, way up high on the top shelf. Nobody ever goes in there. I thought it would be safe."

"Who told you to buy it, Allan?"

"I got a letter in the mail with no name on it. It was written on a prescription form from my brother William. It said he needed it for research purposes. When I talked to him about it when we got back, he told me he didn't send it and knew nothing about it."

"Do you still have the note?" Latimer asked.

"No, it said on the note to throw it away, so nobody would get into trouble." Allan leaned back in his chair. "I wished I had kept it. Maybe that would get me out of here." His orange suit looked crumpled, like he had slept in it. He had lost weight.

"Was it a typed or handwritten note?"

"It was typed with no signature underneath. I wondered about that. I would've thought William would have the decency to sign it, but he didn't. I got the letter a day before we left and didn't have time to call him."

"What exactly did the note say?" Latimer asked. "Do you remember the words?"

"It just said to stop and ask a medicine man for some medicine they use in their tribe to help people with pain. He never asked for stuff to kill anybody. That's why I got it. I thought I was helping." Allan sat and held his head in his hands. "If I tell the police they will arrest William. I can't do that. He says he didn't send the note. Then two of us would be in jail."

"Did anyone threaten you not to tell, Allan?" Latimer asked carefully so as not to make him stop talking.

"I got a phone call right after Dad died, not to ever say anything about this to the police or he would kill me, too." He sounded scared.

"Was it a man or a woman?"

"It was a man I think, but the voice was disguised. It could've been a woman."

"What exactly did they say?"

"Just what I told you. He would kill me if I told anyone."

"Do you still have your cell phone?" Latimer asked.

"The call didn't come on my cell phone. I got a note to go to the Glenridge Mall and wait by the public phone."

"Do you still have that note?"

"No, he said to throw it away or he would go to the police." Allan looked tired. "I did that because I didn't want to go to jail. It didn't work, did it? I'm here."

"How do I know you're not making all this up, Allan?" Latimer asked with steel in his voice.

"I'm not making it up. I'm too tired to make stuff up. I want to get out of this place." He sounded desperate.

"Would you agree to talk to the police about it without your lawyer?"

"I think I'm about ready. My lawyer tells me they don't have anything on me and to wait for the trial. I won't last in this place until the trial." He was crying. "I want to go home. I didn't do anything wrong."

Latimer looked at the pitiful young man and didn't know whether to believe him or not. He leaned over and took Allan's hand.

"How do I know you're not putting on this great show for me just to get out of here?" He asked. "Can you give me one solid piece of evidence why I should believe you?"

"My mom knows who the person is who wrote the note. That's why she tried to kill herself. She knows I'm innocent, but doesn't want to let anyone know who really did it." He had stopped crying.

"How do you know that, Allan?"

"She told me. That's why she tried to kill herself. She didn't want to have two of us in jail." He looked at Latimer with new hope in his eyes. "She knows and she can tell you. Go talk to her."

Latimer knew he was telling the truth now. It confirmed what he had thought all along, ever since Patricia had tried to kill herself. He would talk to her.

"Allan, the next time you speak to your mother, would you ask her if I can come and talk to her. Tell her, I have something that can help you get out of jail."

"I will do that. I'm allowed to call her collect every day." He got up and knocked on the door for the guard to let him out. "Thanks, Latimer." There was a new tone of humility in his voice Latimer had never heard from him before.

"I will have Det. Sgt. Brighton come and he will interview you, Allan. Make sure you co-operate. Who knows, you may get out on bail," Latimer said before he walked out. "One more thing, Allan, put me on your visitor's list so I can come visit you anytime."

"I will, Latimer," Allan said.

Latimer stopped by Brighton's office and told him what he found out.

"I think you need to follow up on this. That boy is innocent. All he did wrong was to bring a substance into the country he thought was pain medicine for his brother for research. You may have to let him go or at least let him out on bail."

"That means the case is not solved and I'm right back where I was when I started." Brighton groaned. He looked at Latimer with a half-smile. "Where do we go from here, Sir?"

"That is a good question. I'm going to talk to Patricia. Let's see what that brings. If I don't get anywhere with her, you'll have to interrogate her, since Allan says she knows who wrote the note." Latimer got up and walked to the door. "We're a lot closer, Kid. It's better to start over and get the right suspect than have an innocent man sit in jail."

"It doesn't feel better right now. Especially, since I have to go and talk to the Chief and tell him we have the wrong man." He groaned again. "I wish you were back, Latimer."

Later in the afternoon, Patricia Hellman called Latimer while he was back at the office.

"Mr. Latimer, my position has not changed. I will not talk to you about me or anyone else in this family." She sounded adamant.

"In other words, you are ready to let your son Allan rot in jail?" Latimer said in a terse voice. "What kind of a mother are you?"

"Since you don't know the circumstances, you cannot understand why I'm doing this. It is and always has been to protect my children. I don't care what happens to me, I care that they get their inheritance."

"What about Allan? Does he deserve to go to prison for life? Without you clearing things up he definitely will, Ma'am."

"I don't think so, Mr. Latimer. I can afford the best legal team there is. He will be declared innocent, I'm sure of it." She sounded absolutely sure of herself as she hung up.

He wondered what she knew that made her so sure that no one was going to be held responsible for the two murders. Latimer felt frustrated. Maybe the lab boys would find something on the video or the safe deposit box. He was hoping a judge would sign off on the warrant for the ledger.

Shortly after his conversation, he locked up and went home. The weather was still cold and damp. At least it wasn't raining or snowing. He shivered as he got into the car. He had been so sure Patricia would talk to him. The woman had a lot of backbone. Brighton would have to interrogate Dr. Hellman about the note having been written on his prescription form. He was almost certain whoever wrote it, stole it from his office. The man had no motive to kill either his father or the butler. Any of the siblings could have gone to his office and taken the form. This could've happened over a year ago and nobody in the office would remember. Or would they? Maybe he could stop by and ask tomorrow. It wouldn't hurt. Nothing else was working out.

The next morning presented a clear, blue, cold sky. There were icy pockets on the road and he drove careful. He had called and got an appointment with the office manager of Dr. Hellman's practice. She turned out to be an efficient, no nonsense, middle-aged woman, who looked at him as if he were an inconvenient interruption in her busy schedule.

"My name is Lynn Carter. I don't have much time to talk to you, Mr. Latimer. We are busy today. What can I do for you?" She was African-American, with short hair and a trim, figure. Her face looked like she didn't smile easily.

"I need to know if Dr. Hellman's family comes to the practice a lot."

"Why would they do that, Mr. Latimer? They have no reason to disturb him here, unless they see him professionally."

"Did any one of them stop by about a year ago? I know it's a long time, but since visits are rare, you might remember," Latimer asked.

"I can't say I recall." She pondered for a minute. "Wait. There was an occasion a year ago when his mother, his sister Becky and his brother Allan came by for shots before they went to the Amazon. The reason I remember, we had to order the shots especially for them since we don't do that kind of thing." She leaned back in her chair. "There was one other time when his sister Sylvia and his brother Grant came by to pick him up for a meeting. I do remember it well. His brother made a fuss about having to wait for a while. It was very unpleasant for our office staff up front. We finally had them wait in Dr. Hellman's private office to calm him down."

"That is all I wanted to know, Mrs. Carter. Thank you so very much, you've been most helpful." He got up and left.

One of them took a prescription form during that visit. It could've been any of them. He sighed in frustration. This had not exactly been helpful.

Latimer went to the precinct to find out if the lab guys had found any fingerprints on the box. Brighton was sitting in his office in an unusually glum mood.

"The Chief got really ticked off when I told him what you found out from Allan. He yelled at me for having the wrong person in custody. The entire precinct heard it, I'm sure." Brighton tried to suppress his anger. "What did you find out from the mother?"

"Nothing, she won't talk to me. You may have to go and do it. I won't come with you, because it just gets her more upset and determined not to say anything," Latimer said. "Did they get the results of the fingerprints on the box yet?"

"I'm waiting. Inspector Brown has a big case that takes precedent at the moment. He is not going to let me interfere."

"Don't be discouraged, Kid. We'll get it solved. Something always comes up." Latimer looked at Brighton with a smile. "Just when you think things are at its worst, the case unravels. We've been there so many times and this is no different. Don't worry about the Chief yelling at you. He'll praise you to high heaven when we find the killer and tell you how great you are."

Brighton looked at Latimer with a gloomy look.

"I don't know if I can do this for the rest of my career. Maybe I'll just take a quiet desk job without all this stress. I don't know how you did it for thirty years, Latimer?"

The phone rang. It was the fingerprint lab. There were no prints on the box other than Brighton's and Latimer's. It had been wiped clean. When Brighton hung up the phone, a messenger came with the search warrant for the bank ledger. Brighton jumped up and grabbed his coat.

"Let's go to the bank. Maybe we'll find something. Nothing else seems to be working out around here," he said on the way out.

This time they were led into a small conference room. The assistant bank manager, who had taken the ledger before, brought it to them with a smile.

"I'm George Harris. I didn't mean to be uncooperative before, but we value the privacy of our customers at this bank. I hope you find what you're looking for. We're more than happy to work with the police as long as it is by legal means." He put the ledger on the table and left the room.

"Well, let's see if we can find a familiar name in here. Two sets of eyes are better than one," Latimer said. He put the ledger between them on the table and began scanning the rows of names. It proved to be more difficult than they imagined since the names were entered by each customer in their own handwriting. They scanned from the most recent on backwards for about fifteen minutes.

"Here it is. Patricia Hellman. She took whatever was in there right after Henry was murdered," Latimer said. "I wonder how she managed to get to the box. We need to ask what the bank policy is for taking out the contents of anyone's safety deposit box."

Brighton and Latimer found George Harris in his office upstairs.

"We found the person who took the contents," Brighton told him. "It was not the owner. Can you tell me the procedure of who was allowed to open Mr. Gossomer's box, Mr. Harris?"

George Harris looked at Patricia Hellman's name.

"I do remember the lady. She came with a signed note from Mr. Gossomer, which gave her authorization to open it and take out the contents. Since it was signed and notarized, we did not see any reason why we should not comply."

"What did she look like?" Latimer asked.

"She was in her late fifties, early sixties, very distinguished and well dressed. She said the man was her butler and she was doing this as a favor to him since he was very ill. I saw no reason to suspect her of any wrongdoing, Sir." He was beginning to look nervous. "Is there anything wrong?"

"Not yet, Mr. Harris," Brighton said. "We are still looking into it and may need to talk to you again."

"Certainly, any time Det. Sergeant. I'm always willing to cooperate with the police as I stated before." He was nervous now.

"It was Patricia Hellman," Brighton said. "That woman is getting more and more mysterious. Now I know I'm going to have to go and talk to her about this. I want you to come with me, Latimer. I don't care if she doesn't like it, she won't have a choice." He sounded determined.

Chapter 20

The next morning Latimer went directly to the precinct to ride with Brighton to the interview with Patricia Hellman. A new butler introduced himself as Paul Weinberger and showed them into the family room.

Patricia was sitting in her favorite chair overlooking the wintry landscape through the big window. She held a coffee cup in her hand. Without getting up to greet them she pointed to two chairs without saying a word.

"Thank you for seeing us, Mrs. Hellman," Brighton said with a big smile. "I hope you're feeling better after your ordeal in the hospital."

"Get to the point. I don't have very much energy yet, Det. Sergeant," she said without taking her eyes off the view outside.

"We examined the ledger at the bank and know you took out the contents of Henry Gossomer's bank deposit box. May we ask what was in it?" He sounded friendly.

"I have no intentions to talk to you unless you want to arrest me." Her voice was flat and lifeless.

"I will have no other choice to do just that, unless you answer our questions, Mrs. Hellman," Brighton answered. "I really don't want to do that, given your delicate condition."

"My life means nothing to me, Detective. It is my children who are important. Whatever I do or don't do is for them and no one can fault me for that. Last I heard, that is not against the law." She sounded disinterested.

Latimer leaned forward and looked at her.

"Mrs. Hellman, I talked to Allan. He is profoundly unhappy sitting in jail and begs you to talk to me, so he can be released on bail. He insists you know who the killer is."

"I know all about Allan. He will have to stick it out till the trial. I'm certain he will be declared innocent," she said without emotion.

"How do you know that?" Latimer asked.

"I just do." She continued to stare outside. "Do you see those empty, bare trees out there, Mr. Latimer? That is me. I feel empty and bare and it is my husband's fault. He is the one who ruined this family. I hate him. I hate what he has done to me." Her voice was totally void of emotions. "I wish they would have let me die. Go ahead, arrest me. I don't care about anything anymore." She looked at Latimer with a cynical smile. "What good are fifty million dollars when all I feel is emptiness?"

"Would it not help if you talked about what is bothering you, Mrs. Hellman? Sometimes it feels good to say out loud what we bottle up inside." Latimer asked in a gentle tone. "We will find out the truth anyway. It may take us a little longer if you don't tell us, but we will find it."

"I know. I just want to pretend right now that everything is the way it always was and my children are safe. That is the least I can do for them." She looked at Latimer with profound sadness. "You cannot help me, Mr. Latimer. Nobody can."

They knew there was no need to ask her anything else. She had retreated into her world of silence as she stared out into a seemingly cold and dead world outside.

"I don't think I've ever seen anyone this unhappy, Latimer," Brighton said when they drove off. "I have a feeling this lady isn't going to live very much longer."

"I think you're right and there is nothing we can do to help her. Even if we find which one of her children killed her husband and Henry, she will be all the more sad to see them go to prison. What a terribly tragic situation." Latimer felt deeply touched.

"It makes me want to strangle the lazy, greedy kid who did this to her. I'm determined to find him or her just to get justice for this lovely lady." Brighton sounded angry and determined. He turned to Latimer. "Do you have any idea who it could be?"

"I don't, Brighton. After all this time, I still don't know who poisoned these two people. Unless something happens to brake open the case, we may never know. The least of my worry is that the kids don't get their money for ten years. They all deserve to wait, if you ask me." Latimer felt emotionally drained after the sight of Patricia Hellman. He had never seen anyone so broken.

When they arrived at the precinct, they sat in Brighton's office in silence for a while, still shaken from the meeting.

"I don't know where to go from here," Latimer finally said. "We've hit a stone wall. I checked Dr. Hellman's office to see which of the kids visited there a year ago in order to steal one of the prescription forms. Every one of them was there at that time, according to the manager."

"I don't know what to do now either." Brighton sounded dejected. "The Chief will be upset with me and demand some action. If I can't come up with anything, this will go to the cold case files. Since you can't solve it Latimer, no one can. Even the Chief will admit to that." He looked at Latimer with pleading in his eyes. "You wouldn't want to go with me to tell him, would you?"

"One of the biggest reasons I like being retired Brighton, is the fact, I don't have to answer to that man anymore. I remember his booming voice vividly, telling me in so many words, I was getting too old for the job." He looked at Brighton with empathy. "I understand how you feel, but part of your job is to learn to stand up for yourself and let, whatever the Chief throws at you, roll off your back. If you have done all you can, then that is going to have to be good enough for the Chief. The important thing is not to let his accusations take away your self-worth." Latimer leaned forward. "One of the things that helped me was a question I would ask him when I was in a fix like this."

"What was it?" Brighton looked at him with hope.

'What would you suggest I do, Chief?'

"Since he doesn't have a clue what that is, it usually makes him stop yelling. There were five times in my career I had to give up and let a case go to the cold files. It is not the end of the world, Kid. What it does do, is make you try harder with the next one. Every one of those five cases happened when I first started out, just like you are. The difference between you and me now is that I have the luxury to keep on digging, you don't." Latimer got up and walked to the door. "That is exactly what I'm going to do and I will let you in on what I find." He smiled. "The fat lady hasn't sung yet, Kid. Keep your chin up. We are going to solve this case."

Latimer wished he was as sure about that as he sounded. He drove back to his office, not knowing what to do next. He could always go home and sit in front of the fireplace and dream of retirement in Florida.

Chapter 21

Two months passed. Allan Hellman's trial was about to begin. The local media had picked up the case and would be there in force. Latimer was not any closer to finding the real killer. All he knew, Allan either didn't do this alone or he was totally innocent. Brighton had been assigned to another case. For all intents and purposes, the case had been solved and the murderer was behind bars.

Gary Norton had called the other day to find out if Latimer was still working on it. If Allan was convicted, he was prepared to pay out the inheritance to the children and pay Latimer's fee. For a second, Latimer was ready to collect and let things go. But his conscience would not allow him to take the money, knowing he didn't do anything to prevent an innocent man going to prison.

It was a Monday morning. He decided he would go visit Allan in jail and see if there was anything new he might find out. Latimer had no idea what it would be. He called it fishing. You never knew what might get caught in the net, if you looked for it and asked the right questions.

Allan looked terrible.

"Hi Latimer, I'm surprised you still come and see me. No one else does. I'm stuck in this hellhole without hope." He had lost a lot more weight. His face had a grayish color to it and there were dark rings under his eyes. "You're the only one who cares enough to visit me, except my lawyers. I have a feeling they don't believe me either."

"How about your mother, Allan, has she not come by?"

"She's too sick to leave home. I call her collect every day and she sends me money so I can buy the things I need in here." His eyes looked dull and lifeless.

"Has she said anything that might tell us who killed your father and Henry?"

"I asked her, but she won't talk to me about that. All she ever says is that I will be found innocent. When I ask her how, she tells me to wait and see. I can't figure it out."

Latimer noticed Allan had changed. He had stopped whining. Instead, there was a strange calm in his demeanor. Latimer knew the man had been through rough times in that place. Gone was the immature boy. What was left was a man who had been seasoned by three months of terrible cruelty.

"What can I do to help you, Allan?" he asked him.

"There is nothing anyone can do for me." He sat with his head in his hands. "I was a spoiled, foolish, immature boy who hung onto his mother's apron strings. Now look at me. I feel I've lived a lifetime in the months I've been in here. My father's video runs through my head like a loop. His words, that I'm too spoiled to function in the real world, are no longer true. He wanted me to help others so I could see how the rest of the world lived. Well, Latimer, his wish has come true. I'm seeing every day how horrible life can be. There are people in here who have never had anything but hardship and tragedy. Their parents beat them and life treated them cruelly in ways I cannot even imagine. I'm not surprised they are in here and treat each other with the same hatred as they've been treated. That's all they know."

"What are you saying, Allan?" Latimer asked.

"For the first time in my life, I'm able to look past my own nose and see the suffering, cruelty and pain other people go through and call it living. I sit in my cell, together with three other people, and hope none of them decide to hurt me when I close my eyes. They know I'm a spoiled, rich brat and they hate me for it. I'm at their mercy and there is no one to help me. I'm trying to understand what makes them tick, while all they see is my money. What they don't understand, all my money does me no good if I'm found guilty. I'll end up in prison just like they will." He looked at Latimer with great sadness. "I wonder what my dad would think of me now. He did say I could be a good person. I wonder why? I've never done the first good thing in my whole life." He raised his head and looked at Latimer. "If I should ever get out of here, I will be a different man. I don't know how yet, but I will be what my father saw I could be."

"I haven't given up on you, Allan. I'm still on the case." Latimer tried to sound positive.

"That's nice, Latimer. I hope you solve it and find out which one of my other rotten siblings is a murderer. Don't you see how ridiculous this is? My father must've been sick to his stomach looking at his selfish, lazy and greedy kids. We all stood against him when he tried to make us into responsible human beings." He wiped the tears from his eyes. "I wish I could tell him he was right and we were wrong, but it is too late."

The guard came in and waved for Allan to leave. Visiting time was over.

"Don't give up, Allan. I will find a way," Latimer said with emphasis and shook his hand. "I'm proud of you. You're becoming a man in spite of this place."

When he walked out into the sunlight, Latimer had a new resolve to continue with this case. He would not let this young man go to prison. He was convinced Allan was innocent. Yet he had no idea how, with no new lead and no way of knowing how to solve this case. What he did have, was a new resolve justice would be done. He would see to it.

When he got back to the office, Sue Ellen told him a man named Paul Weinberger had called. The name sounded familiar, but Latimer couldn't place it.

"Did he say why he called?"

"He says he is the new butler at the Hellman's," Sue Ellen said. "He sounded worried somehow. He left a number for you to call him. It's his cell phone. He also said you should call him after seven in the evening when he is off duty." She handed him the slip with the number.

"That's interesting. I wonder what he wants." Latimer vaguely remembered a man in his early forties, who looked very much like Henry with his black hair and erect stature.

"There is someone who wants to hire you to look for a missing person," Sue Ellen interrupted his thoughts. "They left a number for you to call. I told them you were still on a case, but you would get in touch with them." She looked at Latimer with a questioning look. "Or have you given up? We can't be the greatest detective agency in Glenridge if you do that, darlin'."

"We're not giving up, Sue Ellen. This call from the butler might just be the new lead we need. I'm convinced Allan Hellman is not guilty. As long as I have anything to do with it, he is not going to prison for something he didn't do." Latimer sounded energized. "I might as well go play bingo and shuffleboard in Florida if I allow that."

"That's the Latimer I know," Sue Ellen said and gave him a big, encouraging smile. "Should I call them back and say you're not available?"

"You do that."

It was eight o'clock before Latimer had the chance to call Paul Weinberger.

"Mr. Weinberger, this is Robert Latimer. I'm returning your call. What can I do for you?"

"Thank you, Sir. I need to speak with you about an urgent matter. Is there any way you can see me in your office tomorrow? It is my day off and I will be in town."

"Can you tell me what this is about?"

"I would rather see you in person, Sir." He sounded tense.

"I will be in the office by nine. If you can come then that would be great," Latimer said. "I will make sure we're not disturbed."

"I will be there, Sir." He hung up before Latimer could ask any more questions.

"I wonder what this is all about," he said to Glenda. "He is new on the job. What is it that he would know about the case?"

"Maybe he has found something in Henry's room. It's his now, I'm sure," she said. "Remember, this weekend is Peter's birthday party. We're supposed to be there by six for dinner. It sounds like fun. Andrea said Peter's brother Joshua will be there. We haven't seen him since the last case. She told me he's working at the trucking company now. He must've straightened out his life. Maybe he's just decided to grow up."

"The problem with growing up is, just when you have accumulated enough brains to do it, you're too old to use it. Look at me. I wish I knew what I know now when I was young. It reminds me of Brighton. The Kid is eager to do well, but experience is still the one thing that will carry the day in the end. The trouble is, it hasn't done me much good with this case, has it?"

"I have a good feeling about this Paul Weinberger. He sounds like he knows something." Glenda smiled at him. "You're still the smartest and most handsome sleuth I know, Mr. Latimer."

"Since you are the authority on handsome sleuths, I will take your word for it. You may have to adjust your rose-colored glasses a little, though." He laughed. "Everybody needs a cheering section like you, not just smart, but pretty as well." He leaned over and kissed her.

Latimer stepped out into a cold, clear, beautiful morning the next day. He had high hopes for the interview with Paul Weinberger. Maybe this was the turning point he had been waiting for. Sue Ellen had the coffee ready for him.

"Latimer darlin', this is going to be a good day. I can feel it. It's like a coon dog pickin' up on a fresh trail." She looked pretty this morning.

"How's your engagement going? Any wedding bells in the making?" Latimer asked with a smile.

"We're going to get hitched in June. The wedding will be at his parent's church with the reception at their house since my folks live too far away."

"Is your family going to attend?"

"I sure hope so. When this case is finished, we want to take a drive down to Adell and see them. So you better hurry up and get it done, Latimer darlin'," she said with a big smile.

The front door opened and Paul Weinberger walked in. He was dressed in a brown, heavy overcoat. His black hair was fuller than Henry's had been. In his early forties, he was a younger version of Henry Gossomer.

"Come on in, Mr. Weinberger," Latimer said as he came out of his office to greet him. "Can Sue Ellen get you a cup of coffee?"

"That would be nice, Sir. It is mighty cold out there." He followed Latimer into his office. They sat in front of the desk, facing each other. Latimer was glad Sue Ellen had bought the nice desk and matching chairs.

"This is an unexpected surprise, Mr. Weinberger," Latimer said. "I can't imagine what it is I can do for you."

"I think it will be more what I can do for you, Mr. Latimer," he said as he hung his coat on the new coat hanger in the corner. "I am Henry Gossomer's nephew and I took the job at the Hellman's in order to find out who killed my uncle." He looked at Latimer with a smile. "While I am a real butler by profession, I gave up my job and applied for this one in order to see if I could find Uncle Henry's killer. I am the only relative he had. My parents died many years ago and I lived with him from the time I was fourteen. I loved him like a father and he made it possible for me to attend the right school to become a butler. They are not easy to get into, but with his recommendation, I was accepted."

"I must say this is a total surprise. Do the Hellman's know who you are?" Latimer asked.

"They do not. I worried they might suspect something, since I look very much like my uncle, but in that house, no one pays much attention to the servants." He sounded cynical.

"I gather you don't like it there?"

"I don't, Mr. Latimer. I had a very good position. My former employer knows about my so-called assignment and will take me back when it is done." He smiled. "I hope it doesn't take too long."

"Why come to me, Mr. Weinberger?"

"I know you have been hired by the late William Hellman to look into his murder. I figure, since the same person who murdered him also murdered my uncle, we have a common goal."

"That sounds great to me." Latimer took a sip of his coffee. "Have you found anything interesting pertaining to the case since you've worked there?"

"I've spent my time evaluating which one of the children has the motive and intelligence to pull something like this off. My conclusion is, all of them. However, not all of them are inclined to do something horrible like murdering two people in cold blood."

"Do you think Allan is guilty?" Latimer asked him.

"No, I don't. While he is the worst of the lot to live with, he is not a murderer. To me he is a pathetically spoiled child in a man's body. His mother has seen to that."

"You would be amazed how much he has grown up since he's been in jail," Latimer said. "I talked with him yesterday and I was astounded at the change. There is hope for him."

"Really? I would not have thought he would be capable of changing." Paul Weinberger put his cup down on the desk.

"Jail has a way of making or breaking a man," Latimer said. "I've seen it happen more than once in my thirty years on the force. Allan is becoming a man and it is encouraging to see."

"That is wonderful. I would be very happy to see him grow up."

"Which one of the children do you think has done it, Mr. Weinberger?" Latimer asked.

"Please call me Paul. I'm more comfortable with that."

"Then you must call me Latimer, everybody does."

"To answer your question, I think it is Sylvia or Grant, or both. I have seen them huddled together and whispering so their mother can't hear. Both have spent a lot of time in Mr. Hellman's room looking for something over the last few weeks. From what little I could hear, they have both acted like they know more than they let on. Once I overheard them telling their mother not to say anything to anyone."

"How is she doing these days? I know she's not well," Latimer said.

"She never recovered from her attempted suicide. From what I can tell, she does not want to live. It is as if she's waiting for the trial and when it's over, she'll die." He leaned back in his chair and sighed. "It is a sad thing to see anyone like that."

"Has she said anything about Allan being in jail?"

"She sends him money and tries in every way to make his life easier while he's there, but she does not talk about him."

"Why did you come here today to talk to me, Paul? You could have told me a long time ago. Why today?" Latimer leaned forward.

"I am torn between my duty to my employer and to my uncle. I would like to share with you what I hear and know is going on in that house. At the same time, I have signed a contract to the effect that I will not divulge anything I hear or see. It is a dilemma I don't know what to do about. Coming here is the first step to figure out what is the best solution." He shifted uncomfortably in his chair. "There are certain things I've come across and have heard that could shed some light on who killed Mr. Hellman and Uncle Henry. All of it is conjecture without proof. However, I figured since you have been hired to find the truth, if we put together what I know and what you have found out so far, it may be enough to solve the mystery. I am considering hiring a lawyer to tell me how to handle this."

"I understand your dilemma, Paul. Maybe the two of us could talk to Gary Norton, the family lawyer. He could definitely tell you what you can share and still honor your contract. It seems to me, if there is a crime involved, the contract would not have to be adhered to in every detail of what you can share with me. I can have my secretary give him a call and make an appointment for us. He is as interested as you and I to solve the case. Since it involves my assignment, I'm sure the estate would pay for the consultation."

"That sounds great, Latimer, I will wait for your call. Give me a day advance so I can take the time off." He stood up and held out his hand. "Thank you, Sir. I am glad I came and talked to you. I hope between us, we can solve this case. It would mean everything to me to put the person away who murdered my Uncle Henry. He was the only family I had."

"Do continue to keep your eyes and ears open, Paul. You are in the perfect place to find the kind of evidence we need," Latimer said as he showed him to the door. "I will be in touch with you. Please, leave your cell phone number with my secretary and the best time to call you."

"That would be in the evening after seven when I'm off work. Don't call during the day. I won't be able to talk."

Latimer looked thoughtful after Paul had left. He wondered what he had that could shed light on the case. The trial was scheduled to begin next week. From what little Latimer knew, all the defense had was circumstantial evidence. Allan's lawyers wanted to involve Becky as a possible suspect, since she had been with him in the Amazon, but Allan wouldn't allow it. He swore she had nothing to do with it, other than doing him a favor by putting the poison in her suitcase. They even suggested Dr. Hellman's complicity, because of the prescription form, but again, Allan told them he did not have anything to do with it. The big question remained who took the poison after Allan brought it home and put it in his medicine cabinet? The defense had only Allan's word that he couldn't find it after his father died. It was a very weak defense and wouldn't convince any jury of his innocence.

As for Latimer, he believed what Allan said, but that wouldn't help, unless he could discover the real murderer. To do that, he needed Patricia to tell what she knew, but she wasn't talking. She remained the only witness to clear Allan's name. Since she was his mother, her testimony would not be of any use without proof. Paul Weinberger was his only chance to get at the truth. He hoped Gary Norton could help by telling the butler, it was legally possible for him to break his contract, since a murder investigation was involved.

Latimer heard Sue Ellen on the phone with Gary Norton's office.

"They will see you on Thursday morning, Latimer," she said as she hung up.

"That sounds good. It will give him two days to arrange his schedule."

Chapter 22

Paul Weinberger arrived promptly at ten on Thursday morning and Latimer drove him to the lawyer's office.

"I appreciate you doing this for me, Latimer," he said. "I was in a real quandary as to know what to do about all this. I am a man of principles and take my job very seriously."

"I'm sure Gary Norton will be able to clarify what you can and cannot do or say," Latimer said as they walked into the door.

"Good morning, Gentlemen," Gary Norton said as he met them in the front office. "Come with me. I don't have much time, but I think I can clarify your position, Mr. Weinberger. He walked down the hallway to his office. "Have a seat." He pointed to two chairs in front of his desk.

After Paul told him about his situation, Gary Norton leaned back in his chair.

"As I understand it, you signed a non-disclosure contract when you started your employment. Is that right?"

"Yes, Sir," Paul said.

"Did it contain a general language or specifics about what you could or could not talk about?" He leaned forward and looked at Paul.

"I can't say that I read all the fine print, but I do remember Mrs. Hellman telling me she would have to insist I don't ever share what goes on in the house with the media."

"Did she include any other entities that you can recall?"

"No, she didn't." Paul reached in his briefcase and took out the contract and handed it to Gary Norton. "Here, I brought my copy with me. Maybe it will help you."

The lawyer read through the entire document.

"This only involves the media, not any individual. It's a standard contract, not very specific or particularly thorough in its language. I would never have suggested it to her if she had asked me." He smiled at Paul. "That makes it easy for you. As long as you do not talk to reporters, nowhere does it say you can't talk to Mr. Latimer." He pointed to the document. "This contract is quite useless, if you ask me. It would never hold up in court. I will have to speak with her about this when all is said and done and this terrible ordeal is over." He got up and walked around the desk and looked at Latimer. "That was easy, Mr. Latimer. Are you still on the case now that Allan is going on trial? You realize you have fulfilled your duty and the guilty party is being tried. On your word I will send you the rest of your fee and distribute the money to the heirs."

"Mr. Norton, I am convinced Allan is innocent of the charges. As far as I'm concerned, the real murderer is still on the loose. Keep the money until I have delivered him to the police. I could never rest, knowing an innocent person sits in prison while I take your money." Latimer sounded adamant.

Gary Norton looked at him in surprise.

"That is most unusual, Sir. I appreciate your ethics. I will hold on to the check until you say the word. Rest assured this kind of honesty and integrity is rare in today's world. I'm sure you'll never lack clients if this gets around. I'm going to make certain it does." He shook Latimer's hand and then turned to Paul. "I'm totally convinced, between the two of you, you will solve this crime. I wish you all the best." He took Paul's hand. "Have a nice day. Let me know if I can be of any further assistance."

On the way back to the office Latimer and Paul Weinberger discussed where to go from here.

"Is there anything you haven't told me you have found out at the Hellman's, Paul?" Latimer asked. "I have a feeling you are keeping some information back. If we are going to work together, I must insist that we are totally open with each other. It isn't going to work otherwise."

"I want to have some time to think about it." Paul said with a slight hesitation in his voice.

"We don't have that much time until Allan's trial starts," Latimer said. "Once he is convicted by a jury, it takes forever to undo it if he is found innocent later by something I find out. I promise you, I will keep it confidential."

"That's not my problem. I have a feeling the person who did this is watching me. If they find out I'm Henry's nephew, I could be in real danger." Paul sounded stressed.

"I hadn't thought of that," Latimer said. "You may be right. We do need to be real careful. That's why it's important you share all information with me. If anything happens, I will understand how to help you."

"Let me think about it. I will get in touch with you tomorrow or the day after and let you know what I've decided."

Latimer felt frustrated, but couldn't do anything. He remembered how Henry had told him over the phone he had something to share and then he never got the chance. He sighed deeply.

"Don't wait too long, Paul. You could be in real danger. It would be better if we did this together."

Paul did not answer.

The next day Latimer got a call from Becky Hellman.

"My goodness Becky, how are you? You sound great."

"They let me go yesterday, Latimer. Getting dried out was probably the hardest thing I've ever gone through, but I haven't had a drink and I won't. I want to thank you again for what you did for me. I'm going to find an AA meeting close to my place. I never want to get in that kind of mess again. I found out I had to admit I'm an alcoholic and that I will always be one, even if I never take another drink. I've learned a lot about myself and what I want to do with my life." She sounded bubbly and happy. "I'm signing up for law school as soon as I get settled. It's not just to please my dad, but his video has a lot to do with it."

"You sound wonderful, Becky. Don't hesitate to call me if you ever feel you need to talk or think you're getting in trouble. I'll always be here for you."

"That's not the only reason I called you. I have something you might want to know. I can't tell you over the phone. Can I come by this afternoon?"

"Of course you can. I'll be here waiting for you."

"Ok. I'll see you then." She hung up.

It was after three when Becky walked in the door. Latimer was stunned at the way she looked. Her eyes were bright and alert. She didn't wear any make-up, but it looked great on her. With her blond hair in a pony tail and a bright smile, she looked almost like a teenager.

"Hello, Latimer. It is so good to see you." She flung her arms around his neck. "I thought about you a lot and what you said when I was in the rehab clinic. You remind me of my dad and how my relationship with him could have been."

Latimer was beaming. He felt like a proud father, welcoming his daughter home.

"Come on in, Becky. Sit down and talk to me." He turned to Sue Ellen. "Becky, this is my secretary Sue Ellen."

The two looked at each other and smiled.

"Can I fix y'all a cup of coffee?" Sue Ellen asked.

"That would be nice, thanks," Latimer said and pointed to a chair for Becky to sit down. "What is it you want to talk to me about?"

Becky waited until Sue Ellen had sat down the coffee cups and left the room.

"I want to keep this quiet, Latimer, because I could be wrong," she finally said. "It would be terrible if I said something that would hurt an innocent member of my family."

"What is it, Becky?" Latimer said in his most gentle tone.

"After I got out of the clinic, I went to see my mom. She looks terrible. It is as if someone has taken her soul and left the body behind, like an empty shell. She told me she doesn't want to live anymore and started to cry. I just sat there and didn't say anything for a while. Then I asked her if she knew who killed Dad and Henry. That's when she looked at me with the strangest look and said, "The person who did this doesn't deserve to live and I will see to it they suffer the consequences." There was hatred in her eyes. I asked her who she was talking about, but she wouldn't say anymore." Becky looked at Latimer with a strange look in her eyes. "I think she was talking about Grant."

"What makes you say that?" Latimer leaned forward with interest.

"Like I said, when I got out of the clinic I went home to see Mom. Since I have a key I walked into the house unannounced and overheard a heated conversation with Mom and Grant. He was yelling at her and demanded to know if she had talked to anyone."

"What did he say exactly, Becky?"

"He was very angry and yelled, "I will not allow you to tell anyone, do you hear me? It would destroy too many people, including me. You have no right to do that and I will make sure you don't."

"I was standing in the hallway out of sight, but I could see them," Becky said. "He put both of his hands on her shoulders and shook her and said again, "You will not tell anyone. Do you have any idea what this would do to me? Things are bad enough as they are, you don't need to make it any worse."

"Mom just stood there and cried and didn't say anything. She sat down in her chair and stared out the window." Becky looked devastated. "Grant is my favorite of all my siblings. I would hate to see him in prison for the rest of his life. At the same time I can't let Allan be sent away if he's innocent." She looked at Latimer, confused. "What a choice. It almost makes me want to drink again to make the pain go away." She dabbed her eyes with a tissue Latimer had handed her.

"You know alcohol will not help. You did the right thing coming to me with this." He looked at her with concern

"Before you go Becky, how did you manage not being seen by Grant and your mom when you went home and overheard them?' Latimer asked.

"I slipped back out the front door and rang the door bell, so no one would know what I heard. Then I pretended I had just arrived."

"I see. Are you sure you'll be alright staying alone in your apartment?" he asked. "Maybe it would be better if you went and stayed with someone for the time being."

She thought for a moment.

"I could stay with Mom and help her deal with this," she said with a sudden resolve. "That way both of us can help each other." She stood up. "Latimer, thank you. You always know the right things to say." She hugged him before she walked out.

"Let me know if you find out anything to solve the case, Becky," he said as he opened the door to the outside for her.

"She's a pretty thing, ain't she?" Sue Ellen said. "I hope she's not the murderer."

"I seriously doubt that." Latimer said, thoughtfully.

An hour later, Paul Weinberger called Latimer on his cell phone.

"I have decided to talk to you and share what I know. I have taken the afternoon off today. Could I come by in fifteen minutes?"

"Absolutely, Paul. Come on, I'll be here waiting for you." Latimer felt upbeat. Things were beginning to start rolling again.

Paul came in with a serious look on his face.

"I feel terrible doing this to my employer, but to get justice is why I work at the Hellman's. I'm glad the lawyer helped me with the legality of this," he said as he sat down in front of Latimer's desk.

"Now then, what is it that you found that could shed some light on this case, Paul?"

Paul reached into his jacket breast pocket and took out a crumpled envelope and handed it to Latimer.

"I found this in my uncle's room wedged in the back of the chest-of-drawers. I think this is what he died for."

Latimer took the envelope and opened it slowly. In it was a piece of paper, torn out of a binder and folded in half. After he finished reading it, he looked at Paul and said, "I believe you're right. This is what he died for." He laid it on his desk carefully and leaned back in his chair. "Do you have any idea who wrote this, Paul?"

"I don't, but I think it was Grant. It seems to be a part of a notebook.

"Why do you think it was Grant?"

"It sounds like him, arrogant and selfish, without a thought of how his actions affect others," Paul said without hesitation.

"You may be right," Latimer said and took up the paper and read it again carefully.

I have had enough. My life has consisted of waiting for the right time to do as I have always wanted to. To refuse sharing in the wealth that is ours is cruel. It is time now to make it possible for me to set things straight in this area. I have decided to remove the only hindrance to my goal in a way nobody will ever find out. I know it is wrong, but it has to be done in order for everyone in the family to live the way we are meant to live. May God forgive me for what I am about to do. I know He will understand, because my motives are good and will benefit us all to live our lives in luxury. The money belongs to all of us, not just one person, and it is my duty to distribute it the only way I know how. William Hellman believes he will go to heaven when he dies. If that is true, he will not miss us or his money after he is gone. No one will ever know who did this and no one will go to jail. Yet all of us will benefit. I am convinced my plan is fool-proof.

"I have a feeling the beginning of this note is missing," Latimer said. "I would like to have this dusted for fingerprints, Paul. I still have friends at the precinct. They'll do it for me if you don't mind. Since most of the Hellman's fingerprints are in the database, we may just find out who wrote this," Latimer said as he folded it back up.

"Do you think it is Grant?" Paul asked.

"I don't know. It could be any one of them."

"In my opinion, there is no one more self centered and arrogant than Grant. According to the rest of the staff, he came around a lot before Mr. Hellman was killed under the pretense of caring."

"Did he do that before this happened?"

"They told me he rarely came by, and then only, when he wanted money from his father. If he didn't get it, his mother would give it to him. One way or the other, he always had an ulterior motive for showing up, until about two weeks before Mr. Hellman died."

"He told me he was the only one in the family close to your uncle for many years. Do you know if that is true?" Latimer asked.

"Uncle Henry told me many times, no one in the family except Mr. Hellman, ever paid any attention to him or the staff, except to give them orders or yell at them." Paul sounded sure.

"Grant could've lied to me when I spoke to him to make me rule him out as a suspect," Latimer said, rubbing his beard. "In any case, he seems to have lied about that little detail."

"How about Sylvia? Did he ever mention her in any way?"

"I remember him telling me she was harsh, mean and stand-offish, not just with the staff, but with everyone. He said there was much anger inside her, especially against her father," Paul said.

"Did the staff say anything about Dr. Hellman, the oldest?"

"He came around regularly and was always a gentleman, they said. He would sit with his father and talk to him more than the others. There seemed to be no hard feelings between them toward the end. They thought the two of them had made their peace."

That did not sound at all what William had told Latimer, when he interviewed him. He had heard a lot of resentment in his voice about his father not spending any time with him. However, William never complained about the money like the others.

"I think I'll have to agree with you. It sounds like Grant is the most likely one left to have written this note and the one who killed his father. They have his fingerprints in the database at the precinct. It will be very easy to find out if this is his note. It seems to have been part of a diary or a notebook, as if to write out a plan of action on how to commit the murder." Not very smart if you plan to kill someone, Latimer thought; yet Grant was a very smart man. Latimer stroked his beard again.

"I have to think about this some more. We would hate to put another innocent man in jail." He smiled at Paul. "I will take it from here and go to the precinct after our meeting. By Monday morning we should have the results." He got up and showed Paul out. "I will definitely let you know what they find."

Before Paul walked out he turned to Latimer.

"I almost forgot, Grant is making his mother take valium. He comes every day and gives it to her. I think that is why she acts so strange."

On his way home, Latimer dropped the note off at Brighton's office. He was looking forward to a nice weekend.

Chapter 23

Paul Weinberger drove home after he left Latimer's office. He felt uneasy and wondered if he had done the right thing, coming here to find his uncle's killer. After all, the murderer had already killed two people and wouldn't hesitate to do the same to him. His stomach tightened into a knot as he drove up to his parking spot in the back of the house. It was beginning to get dark as he walked into the side entrance and up to his room.

It was quiet inside. Dinner had not yet been served. Mrs. Hellman was probably in her room. He listened for any noise from the kitchen, but all was quiet. That was strange. Mrs. Weber, the cook, should be in there fixing the evening meal. Paul stopped before going up the stairs and went to the kitchen instead. It was empty of all signs of food being prepared. He looked into the walk-in pantry. Nothing. Slowly, he walked to the family room. There was no one there. As he climbed the stairs to Patricia Hellman's room, a feeling of impending doom came over him. He knocked on her door. There was no answer. Carefully, he opened it. Patricia was sitting on the edge of the bed, staring at him with a look of such sadness, it made him take in a sharp breath.

"Mrs. Hellman, why are you here by yourself? Where is everyone?" He asked as he walked over to her.

"I sent them all away. I want to be alone."

"I'm sorry, but I can't leave you alone, you're too upset." He sat in the chair next to the bed. "Why don't we talk about why you're so overwhelmed with grief? Your children are doing well and Allan's trial is beginning on Monday. With the great legal team you have provided, I'm sure he'll be found innocent." Paul was talking to her like she was a child.

"You do not understand, Henry," she said and looked at him with an empty smile. "You don't understand anything."

He did not answer her. She was calling him Henry. Could it be she had lost her grasp on reality?" He wondered.

"What is it I don't understand, Mrs. Hellman," he asked in a gentle tone. "You can tell me."

"I wish I could. You have been with us for so many years. I've never treated you nice, have I? William did, but not the rest of us." She looked down at her folded hands in her lap. "William was good and kind and loved me in spite of the way I treated him. He didn't deserve what he got, but it is too late. Everything is too late." She began to cry. "I wish I could have another chance to do things right. Instead I'm forced to look at myself and see the failure I've been as a wife and a mother."

"We all fail, Mrs. Hellman. That is no reason to give up," Paul said, trying to sound encouraging.

"I'm wondering if I could tell you something, Henry. Would you keep a secret?" She looked at him with a questioning look.

"You can trust me, Madam. Tell me what is bothering you." He held his breath. Would this be what he had been waiting for?

Before Patricia could go on, the door opened and Grant walked in.

"What are you doing here, Paul? You have no business bothering my mother. I thought it was your day off. See to it this doesn't happen again or I will have to dismiss you." His voice was harsh. He looked angry.

"I beg your pardon, Sir. I found Mrs. Hellman alone in the house when I returned this evening. I was worried about her and found her in the bedroom in a bad state." Paul had gotten up from his chair and walked toward the door.

"Did she tell you anything?" Grant's voice sounded menacing. "Did she tell you what she knows?" He stepped in front of Paul to block his way out of the room.

"No, she didn't, Sir." Paul's voice was shaking. He was scared.

"Are you sure?"

"Yes, I'm sure, Sir."

"Mother, have you been telling Paul what you know?" He sounded harsh.

"I was just talking to Henry about things," she said in a feeble voice. "He's been with us for so long, we can trust him. He told me we could."

"I don't know what you're trying to pull, Paul, but don't you ever speak to my mother about private things again. Do I make myself very clear?"

"Yes, you do, Sir." Paul was still unable to leave the room. "May I leave now, Sir?" He asked without looking at the man.

Grant stepped aside reluctantly.

"You watch yourself and make sure you know your place." He walked over to sit with his mother as Paul left the room.

Paul was shaking and realized he had been in the same room with the murderer of his uncle and his employer. He locked the door of his room carefully and sank into a chair. He was scared. On the other hand, five more minutes and he would have found out what it was that had Patricia Hellman so upset. He wondered if she really had dismissed everyone or if Grant had had a hand in that. What if he had planned to kill his mother tonight to keep her from telling anyone that he was the murderer?

Paul knew he had a choice to stay and try to find out more or leave and be safe. He would sleep on it and then decide in the morning. In spite of being hungry, he didn't dare go downstairs to the kitchen as long as Grant was in the house. It looked like he was going to stay for a while.

Suddenly, he heard the front door open. It was Becky. He was relieved.

"Paul, can you come down and help me?" Becky called up the stairs. "I have some luggage I need brought in."

He went downstairs and carried her things into her old room.

"I'm going to stay with Mom, Paul. Neither one of us needs to be alone right now." Becky sounded good.

"That is a wonderful idea, Ms. Hellman. I am sure your mother will appreciate the company," he said as he put the last bag down. "There is no dinner, since your mother dismissed the staff for the evening. Can I fix you something or order take-out for all of you?"

"That sounds wonderful, Paul. Let's ask Grant and Mom what they want."

Grant decided he wasn't going to stay. When he asked Mrs. Hellman, she told him she wasn't hungry. Becky decided on a sandwich of some kind and a glass of hot tea.

"Fix one for you as well, Paul, and we can sit in the kitchen and eat together," she added.

"Very well, Ms. Hellman," he said. It was the first time a member of the family had treated him with kindness. Something must have happened to change Becky Hellman. He wondered what it was as he prepared the sandwiches.

"Thank you for doing this on your day off, Paul," she said as she bit into the sandwich. "I'm hungry. The food in the rehab clinic wasn't that great. I was hoping for a nice meal tonight, but I guess Mom isn't into that. I worry about her." She looked at Paul with sudden interest. "You remind me of Henry. Are you sure you're not related?"

"He was my uncle, Ma'am." He held his breath. There was no sense lying.

"You came to find out who killed him, didn't you?" She sounded curious. "I wish I knew who did it. I know it wasn't Allan. He doesn't have what it takes." She took a sip of the tea. "I think it was Grant. He has been behaving very strange lately, don't you think?" She didn't wait for an answer. "Were you close to Henry?"

"He took me in when my parents died many years ago. He was like a father to me and I was terribly upset when I realized somebody killed him. And yes, I came here to find out who did it." He knew this could be the end of his job.

"Have you found out anything, Paul?" she asked.

"I will have to agree with you. Grant sounds like the most logical choice. Of course there is no proof, but I can't think of any of the others who could've done it," he said. "Would you like some more tea, Ma'am?"

"Thanks, Paul," she said and held out her cup. "I'm still in shock when I think that it is my family we're talking about. My father murdered, the butler poisoned and one of us kids did it. It makes my being an alcoholic seem like nothing." She looked at Paul. "You did know I was in a rehab clinic for a month, didn't you?"

"I did, Ma'am. From what I see tonight, it has done miracles for you. Not only do you look well, but you act different. I don't know what they did in that clinic, but whatever it is, it changed you for the better." He smiled at her. "Your father would be proud of you."

"I do want to make him proud of me, Paul. I will be what he wanted me to be. I'm signing up with a law school in the spring and become a lawyer like he said I should. Hopefully by then this nightmare will be over." She finished up her sandwich. "I am going to try to find out what my mom knows while I'm here. There has got to be a way to get her to talk."

"She almost told me tonight," Paul said, "but at that moment Mr. Grant walked in and asked me to leave the room. He was very upset with me and threatened to fire me if I ever tried to talk to her about anything private again." He took the plates and carried them to the sink. "Your mother thought I was Henry and decided she could trust me."

"You're kidding. Maybe we can try that again when Grant isn't here tomorrow. Now that I'm here, he will probably not come by too often. I'm going to let Mr. Latimer know what happened. He has helped me in many ways throughout all this." Becky got up. "Let's work together on this, Paul. Maybe we can solve this case before Allan is sent to prison."

"That would be wonderful, Ms. Hellman."

Chapter 24

Latimer and Glenda walked into the meeting room of the Glenridge Golf and Country Club. They were one of the last to arrive.

Peter Bellami was beaming. He had his arms around Andrea and was in an animated discussion with Jerry and Cassie. Jerry had just said something and everyone was laughing.

"There they are," Cassie said. "It's about time. We were wondering if you were going to make it." She walked up to Latimer and Glenda and gave them a big hug. "I miss you guys." She looked great in a pair of dress slacks with a loose fitting, colorful top. Jerry followed her and hugged Glenda and then shook Latimer's hand. His jeans and t-shirt looked expensive, certainly not his usual, casual brand. It was clear, Cassie had picked them out.

"We are glad you came. How is the detective business, Latimer?" Jerry asked with his boyish grin. 'Have you caught the bad guy yet? I still remember when you had me arrested. It traumatized me to the point I still have nightmares about it." He grinned as Cassie looked at him disapprovingly. "Don't you go picking on my favorite detective, Jerry," she said, laughing. "You are still my hero, Bob."

"Hey, I'm glad you could come," Peter said as he hugged Glenda. "It wouldn't be the same without you."

"Happy Birthday, Peter," she said with a big smile. "You look great. Fatherhood agrees with you."

"Andrea keeps me straight in that department. Between her and the baby, I've become a real home body these days." He smiled at Andrea.

"Don't believe a word he says. He literally lives at work," she said.

"I have a question for you, Peter," Latimer asked. "Is Barry Henderson still working for you?"

"Yes, he is. As a matter of fact, I have taken him back as VP and he's doing great. I think he has straightened out his life. His daughter moved down and is living with him."

"That is great. I wondered many times if he ever overcame his problems," Latimer said.

"He is still going to a group meeting once a week I think," Peter said. "He is a good man and definitely helps me get my bearings with running the company. We're not friends, but good working partners. I don't know what I would do without him. I still have a lot to learn and he is teaching me."

"How is Jerry juggling between his new life with Cassie and his career at Bellami Trucking?"

"You know Jerry. Nothing much shakes him," Peter said with a smile. "He is what he is. I've never met anyone so unaffected by money or status. He still drives Cassie's little Honda Civic and shows up in jeans and t-shirts just like he always has." He turned to where Cassie and Jerry stood. "I believe they are very happy."

"If it isn't our favorite Inspector and his lovely lady." The voice and accent were unmistakable. Emily walked up to them with a bright smile, her face a multitude of wonderful, tiny wrinkles. Her eyes sparkled. "We miss ye both, don't we Richard?"

"We do indeed. It is so good to see you two," Richard said with a big smile. "It brings back good memories."

"Richard and Emily, how in the world are you?" Glenda said as she hugged both of them. "I need to get that recipe from you for your Irish stew, Emily. Bob is always on me to fix it for him in this cold weather. I'll call you."

Emily was beaming.

"You do that, Glenda dear. It's been handed down from my mother in Ireland."

Latimer spotted Joshua, Peter's brother, at the other end of the table. The young man looked quite different from the insecure, shy and glum person he remembered. Joshua was talking with his mother. He was smiling as he helped her with the hors devours.

"Mom, try this, it's delicious," he said as he put a cracker with some kind of seafood mix on her plate. He looked at her lovingly. A smile crossed his face when he spotted Latimer.

"How very nice to see you, Mr. Latimer. It has been a while since we met."

"You look like a different person, Joshua. I don't have to ask if you're doing well," Latimer said as he walked up to him. "I hear you're working at the company?"

"I am and I must say I enjoy it. I'm trying out each department to see where I fit in. So far I've not made up my mind, but I do like the financial side of the company."

"Maybe you can take over for Mr. Singer one day. Wouldn't that be a relief for everyone?" Latimer said, laughing.

"You would be surprised how that man has changed, Mr. Latimer. He divorced his wife and has become a different person. It made me realize to watch out what kind of girl I date." Joshua said with a big grin. "So far I haven't found anyone I really like."

"Take it from an expert," Latimer said. "Make sure she is as pretty on the inside as she is outside. Just looks won't do if you're searching for the perfect one. Look at Mrs. Singer. I'm sure she was quite beautiful when they started dating, but I guarantee you she was already the shrew then that she ended up being."

"I will remember that." He looked at Latimer with a serious look. "By the way, I never thanked you for what you did for me. I could've ended up in jail if it hadn't been for your understanding and help. Thank you, Sir. I will never forget it." He reached out and shook Latimer's hand. 'We are all grateful for what you did for our family."

It turned out to be a wonderful lunch with delicious food and good friends. Jerry gave a speech in his boyish style and told funny stories about Peter and him growing up. After a toast by everyone, he turned to Cassie.

"I think the lady has an announcement to make."

Cassie rose from her seat and looked at everyone with a big smile.

"Jerry and I are happy to tell you that we are expecting a baby." She took his hand and made him stand next to her. After the shouts of congratulations died down, Jerry said with a big grin,

"It will be a boy and he will come out fully dressed in jeans and a t-shirt." Vintage Jerry.

Chapter 25

Paul Weinberger was on duty over the weekend. He was glad Becky had moved in, because Grant had decided to stay at his mother's for the time being. He never left her side. His behavior towards Paul was harsh and even rude at times. He seemed nervous and on edge with everyone, including the rest of the staff.

Paul had snuck into Patricia's room and checked out her medicine. He found the bottles of tranquilizers, sleeping pills and several other medicines prescribed by Dr. Hellman. It explained to a point why Patricia was in another world most of the time. Her health was frail and she hardly ate anything. Paul assumed she had never gotten over her suicide attempt. Or could it have to do with the many pills Grant was making sure she took every day? He wondered.

Allan Hellman's trial was due to begin on Monday. Grant, Becky and Sylvia had decided to attend. No one told Patricia. The media hype was building up. Paul didn't dare go for fear of being found out. He would have to listen to the local newscast to find out what was going on.

Suddenly, Paul heard loud, angry voices. They came from Patricia's bedroom. It was Becky and Grant. He positioned himself so he could see them through the open door.

"Who are you to tell me what I can and cannot do?" Becky said. "She is my mother, too."

"I told you I don't want you to talk to her. It gets her upset when you ask her questions about Dad," he shouted. "I will not allow you to agitate her with your endless curiosity what she knows. She doesn't know anything. Can't you tell she's out of it?" He sounded angry.

"I know she knows who killed Dad and Henry and so do you. Maybe it was you and you want her to keep quiet about it. Why else are you staying here now that I am back?" Becky's voice was high pitched as she yelled at him. "Why don't you just admit you did it and get it over with? You hated Dad and couldn't wait to get at his money." Becky pointed to the nightstand where the medicine stood. "Why does she need all this stuff?" You're keeping her doped up to make sure she stays quiet." Her voice suddenly changed. She stared at Grant and said in a low, measured tone, "I am absolutely sure you are the murderer. Your behavior has been weird for quite a while." She stared at him with a steely glare. "You murdered our father and Henry and Mom found out about it. You probably helped her with her suicide attempt as well."

"Are you insane?" He screamed and moved toward her with his fist held out. "Be careful what you say or you will regret it you pitiful drunken slut."

Paul decided to enter the room. He cleared his throat and stood respectfully in the door frame.

"Can I be of assistance in any way, Ms. Hellman?' he said.

"Get out, Paul," Grant yelled. "Get out or I will fire you on the spot!"

"You will do no such thing," Becky shouted back. "Thank you, Paul. I'm glad you came in here. My brother is losing it." She sounded calm now and turned to Grant. "You have no right to fire anyone in this house. It does not belong to you. Besides, Mom likes Paul." She stood between Paul and Grant. "I'm going to take over Mom's medication and see to it she is not doped up any longer. If you try to stop me, I will call the police. They would only be too happy to hear from me how you are forcing these pills on Mom." She walked over to the night stand and scooped up the medicine bottles. "I will call William and ask him how much Mom is supposed to have per day."

Grant stood motionless. His face was a mixture of anger and fear. Paul saw his body shake slightly as he tried to control his temper. After a few moments he started to calm down.

"I did not kill Dad and Henry, Becky. For heavens sake, I could never kill anyone, least of all my own father."

"Then why are you so eager to stop Mom from telling me what she knows?"

"Because I know what she knows," he said in a calm voice.

Becky looked at him, stunned.

"How about filling the rest of us in on the secret, big brother? If it isn't because you did it, what could it possibly be you and Mom are trying to hide so desperately?" Her voice was filled with doubt.

"I cannot tell you that and neither should Mom." He was pleading now. "Please, Becky, you have to believe me, it is for the best.

If the secret came out now it would destroy our family even more than we already are. More than that, it would destroy Mom and Allan." He slumped into the big chair beside the bed. "I love Mom and I will do anything to protect her." He looked at Becky and Paul, near desperation in his eyes. "I would even keep her doped up so she won't talk to anyone."

"Why don't I have the right to know what you know?" Becky asked as she sat down in the other chair. "Maybe together we can solve this problem."

"I can't tell you. It wouldn't help if I did, trust me."

"Than tell me something, does it have anything to do with who killed Dad and Henry?" she asked him.

"In a way, but it is much more complicated than that. I've been stressed and upset about this for quite a while now. My nerves are frayed and I'm trying to hold it together. There may be a day soon when everyone can know about it, but just not now." He had composed himself and turned to Paul. "I'm sorry about treating you so mean. Please, forgive me, Paul."

"That is quite alright, Sir. I understand." Paul was trying to decide whether he believed him or not. There were too many unanswered questions. He didn't know if Becky did. If so, he was on his own again. Without a doubt, he would have to continue to get the answer from Patricia Hellman, whether Grant liked it or not.

The trial began on Monday morning. The proceedings were the daily fodder for the media for the next two weeks. Latimer was in attendance every day. He thought Allan held up well as he sat next to his legal team with a stoic expression on his face. The media named him the Amazon Killer. The prosecution focused on a motive of greed, while the defense painted him as an innocent victim, framed by one of his other siblings. In their presentation, they showed him to be the loving son of a grieving mother, who did not have the motive or character of poisoning two people in cold blood. With his youthful, delicate features and good looks, Latimer could tell the jury showed much sympathy for him. They didn't want to believe that this clean cut, young man could possibly resort to such brutality. Especially, since his mother gave him all the money he wanted in spite of his father's objections. There was therefore no need for him to kill anyone, least of all his father and butler. Patricia had hired an excellent, expensive and skilled legal team of three lawyers who didn't miss a single angle to paint Allan as an innocent victim.

The media pointed out that the prosecution had overreached by going for a first degree murder conviction with nothing more than circumstantial evidence. They should have gone for a lesser charge in order to get a conviction. The public was divided whether Allan was guilty or not. They simply enjoyed the three ring circus of the court proceedings, with the outcome anybody's guess.

The Hellman family was represented by one or more member every day. Grant never missed a single time. Paul made it several times, but was prevented by his work schedule to be there every day. He did, however, have a better chance to be alone with Patricia on the days Becky and Grant were gone to the trial. Because of Becky's insistence, Patricia's medicine had been cut back and she was her old self again. She did sit every day glued to the newscast to follow the trial. Her face showed no emotion as she watched. Only when the camera pointed at Allan did she smile, as if to encourage him that everything would be alright.

"They are going to find him innocent, Paul," she would say on a rare occasion. "I know it."

The final day of the trial began with an overcast sky. Latimer was on his way to the courthouse. He had a feeling Allan would be found innocent. Although, one could never know what a jury would do. He had been asked by Becky to sit with the family in the courtroom and arrived early to find the appropriate seat. The place was packed. Every media outlet in the State was scattered with their cameras on the courthouse steps when he arrived. They had come before daylight to get their spot.

There was a hum in the crowd when they led Allan in. Everyone rose when Judge Melissa Carmichael entered. She was a short, tiny woman who looked overwhelmed behind the big desk, until she spoke. In spite of her size, she was in total control of the proceedings and the spectators in the room.

The jury had walked in just before that. Latimer couldn't tell what their verdict would be. All of them kept their eyes down as they took their seat. That could be a bad sign.

The room became silent as Judge Carmichael asked,

"Madam Foreperson, has the jury reached a verdict?"

"We have, your Honor." With that she gave a slip of paper to the clerk. He walked over and handed it to the Judge. She read it without any reaction and turned to Allan,

"Will the defendant please rise."

Allan and his team stood up. Latimer could see he was tense and the color had drained from his face. This was the moment he would find out, whether he would spend the rest of his life in prison or be found innocent. Latimer was nervous and his eyes were glued to the foreperson as she took back the slip of paper from the clerk to read the verdict.

"We the jury, find the defendant Allan Carl Hellman on the charge of first degree murder in the case of William Carl Hellman and Henry Robert Gossomer not guilty on all charges."

Pandemonium broke out in the courtroom. Latimer watched as Allan turned toward his lawyer and hugged him, crying.

"Order in the court," the Judge shouted as she pounded the gavel on the desk. "Allan Carl Hellman," she continued when the crowd had calmed down, "the case against you is hereby dismissed. You are free to go. My thanks to the jury for your time spent." With that she got up and walked out of the courtroom. Latimer could tell she did not agree with the verdict.

Latimer left the courtroom and drove back to his office. Surprisingly, his feelings were mixed. He knew Allan was declared not guilty, but his task remained to find the murderer of William Hellman and Henry Gossomer. At that moment Gary Norton called on his cell phone.

"This is crazy, Mr. Latimer. According to the Will, since the case remains unsolved, I am unable to pay you or the children." He sounded frustrated. "I was sure Allan was going to be convicted. Are you continuing with your investigation, Mr. Latimer?"

"I am, Mr. Norton. Not just that, I believe I know who committed the crime. It will take me a little while to prove it, but now I know. Things have fallen into place after this verdict." Latimer sounded sure.

"Can you tell me who did it?" Gary Norton sounded curious.

"Not until I have proof, Sir."

Latimer smiled. It was an ingenious plan and it had worked. He had no idea how to go about proving it, but he was sure it wouldn't take long. He couldn't help but have admiration for the intelligence and planning that had gone into it. There was not much time left to waste, because he knew the murderer would not take long to disappear. There was no need to stick around, now that the job was done.

Latimer arrived at his office a short while later. Sue Ellen had the day off. He sat behind his desk, stunned and surprised at the simplicity of it all. How could he have missed it all this time?

The phone rang. It was Paul.

"Latimer, I just heard about the verdict. What are we going to do now? I was sure Allan would be convicted in spite of having doubts about his guilt. I feel terribly discouraged. We'll never find out now. I doubt the police will continue to investigate, since they believe he got off because of a foolish, emotional jury." He sounded angry.

"Take it easy, Paul. The police may have given up, but I haven't. As a matter of fact, I will really need your help now more than ever." Latimer took a deep breath. "Listen carefully. This is what I want you to do."

Chapter 26

That afternoon, Patricia Hellman sat in her favorite chair, surrounded by her children. For the first time since the murder, she looked happy. She had her precious son Allan back. Her look fell on him as he sat next to her and she stroked his face.

"I love you, baby. You are free. I told you it would happen."

"I still can't believe it, Mom. You were right." He took her hand and held it. "The time in jail is over and I can live again."

"When are we going to get our money, Mom?" Grant asked when there was a lull in the conversation.

"I heard from Gary Norton," William spoke up. He had come over without his wife. "He called me right after the verdict came out and told me, unless Latimer solves the murder, there will be no money until ten years from now. In other words, nothing has changed until the case is solved." William looked at Grant with disgust. "You just have to wait, little brother, or confess that you did it. Most of us think you did it anyway."

"Stop it you two," Becky said. "We are not going to start that again, are we?"

"Why not, you all still won't get anything until one of us rots in prison." William sounded angry. "I'm truly ashamed to belong to a horrible family like this. Here we are, celebrating the fact that our father's murderer is still running free. As I look at you, any of you could be the one, including Allan. Just because he was found innocent, doesn't mean he is. You did bring the poison from the Amazon, didn't you, little brother?"

Allan looked at William with shame.

"I would like to say something." He stood up and faced the group. "You are right, William. I did that and I am truly sorry. After living through three months of jail I can tell you that I am a different person than what I was then." He stopped until he had everyone's attention. "It is true. I was a spoiled, miserable mama's boy with no other worry than how to get money out of Mom, when Dad wouldn't give it to me. The time in jail and listening to Dad's video changed my life. I am no longer that person. I have seen, just like Dad wanted me to, how the rest of the world lives. The misery, hatred and abuse people in those places have experienced, is unbelievable. I swore, if I ever got out, I would do something to help them. Whenever we get our inheritance, I will see to it that there will be a place in Glenridge for these people when they get out of jail or prison. That's why I want the money as soon as possible. I have every intention to contact New Life Church and talk to the pastor to see if they would be willing to become a part of that kind of outreach. With my money and their volunteers, it could become the beginning of an entire village for the homeless, the needy and those who are destitute." He trembled when he sat back down and tears began rolling down his cheeks. There was a sudden silence as everyone stared at him in surprise.

Patricia began to weep and held his hand.

"Sweetheart," she finally managed to say. "Your father would be so proud of you."

"In other words, you're going to be one of those religious do-gooders?" William said with cynicism in his voice.

"What is wrong with that, William?" Becky said. "What have you ever done with all that money you make other than buying a bigger mansion every year? To criticize Allan, because he wants to change and do what Dad wanted, sounds pretty suspicious to me. You are the one who constantly tells us you don't need Dad's money. I wonder. Before you accuse us of murder, why don't you look at yourself? You are not above suspicion just because you are a doctor." She looked at him with disdain. "Then again, in your profession, doctors take over when God goes on vacation, don't they?"

William's face showed anger as he looked at her.

"I've never needed his money. Unlike the rest of you, I've made something out of my life and I'm proud of it. What that means is, I don't need to be sorry for anything. The fact Dad never talked to me much is not my fault but his. He's the one who was too busy to care about me. Why should I care about what he says on an emotional video he made in order to cleanse his soul. You guys need to get off your duffs and stop whining about your life. Most people wish they had it as good as you." He looked around the room. "One of you killed our father, because you couldn't wait to get his money. I resent being put through the wringer by the police and Latimer and have my integrity questioned. Whoever you are, I have no use for you and hope you rot in prison for the rest of your miserable life. I have nothing more to say." He stood up and walked toward the door. "I'm leaving. This emotional drivel is too much for my taste." Without saying goodbye to his mother, he walked out.

There was silence for a while, until Sylvia spoke up.

"I don't know who might have killed Dad and Henry," Sylvia said. "It is time we found out so we can trust each other again and be a real family." She stood, leaning against the mantle of the fireplace. "No matter what William said, I agree with Allan. Dad's video has had an impact on me as well. I am so sorry I never appreciated him when he was alive. I finally know what I want to do with my life. The wonderful thing is I don't need his money to do it. I can build a business on my own and succeed without it. All of us somehow thought we couldn't live without his millions. I'm here to tell you, we can and we may have to for a long time. We all need to make a choice, either run to Mom or make it on our own. I would rather do the latter." She smiled at them with a look of confidence. "Our father, through his death, left us all a legacy. To some, it will be his money and to others, his love. What he really wanted to leave us, though, is his faith in God so we can make it not only in this life, but to prepare us for a life in eternity. The choice is ours. I will be happy if I can get all three, but if not, the last one will be more than I deserve." She walked over to the couch and sat down.

As if it was her turn, Becky stood up.

"I have just come out of four weeks of rehab. As all of you know, I was a drunk and a lush. Listening to Dad's video made me realize the futility of my empty life. What touched me most was, he loved me in spite of the way I treated him. It is amazing to me that he could still see the good in me and the possibilities hidden underneath my terrible behavior. I have since turned my life around with the help of Bob Latimer and the counselors in the rehab. The first thing I did was acknowledge what a jerk I've been and asked for forgiveness. I have since then turned my life over to a higher power. In my case that is Jesus. After that I had to admit I'm a hopeless alcoholic. Except now, whether to drink or not is my choice and not that of my addiction. More than anything else, I want to change my life and be what Dad knew I could be. I have signed up for the first semester in law school. I'm not ever going to be perfect, but I am determined to be what Dad knew I could be with God's help." She sat down. Everyone looked at Grant, but he didn't say anything.

    Paul had stood behind the half open door of the family room and had heard every word.

Chapter 27

Latimer got to the office early the next morning. Paul Weinberger stood at the front door with a bag in hand.

"Come on in. I will make us a cup of coffee."

Paul handed the bag over to him. In it were several water glasses with a name attached to each.

"That looks great. I will take these to the precinct and have them checked for prints. All I need is one set, but I want to be sure to have them all. The fingerprint lab will compare them with the ones they found on the bottle of poison. If they find the right one, I'll have proof of who the killer is." He put the bag on his desk. "Thanks, Paul. Have a seat and tell me what you heard yesterday."

Latimer was astounded as he listened to the report.

"This is totally amazing. That video William Hellman made has had a profound effect on his children. Even he could not have foreseen that. I'm glad to hear about Allan and his plan. Apparently, he is going through with what he told me when I visited him in jail. It wasn't just words, he really meant it. That's nice. It's the same with Becky and Sylvia."

"That leaves Grant and William," Paul said. "Neither one sounded like they had changed. Especially William was cynical and harsh in his comments. The man has a lot of unresolved resentment in him in spite of his slick exterior as a medical professional." He took a sip of the freshly brewed coffee Latimer had brought him.

"Make sure you keep your eyes and ears open, Paul, even if it takes eavesdropping at the doors. We are getting down to the wire and I don't want to be too late."

"You are sure about your suspicions?" Paul asked.

"I am absolutely certain. Everything fits." He leaned back in his chair. "This has been an unusually sad case in every way. The only bright spot is the fact that some of the kids are turning their lives around, just like William Hellman wanted them to. What a price to pay on his part. Can you imagine turning in one of your own children to be prosecuted for murder, just so they will have a chance to turn their life around?"

"He seemed to have been an unusual man in every way. I wish I could've met him," Paul said. "There is something special about that video. It has had a powerful effect on three of his children. It changed the course of their lives one hundred and eighty degrees. His gamble paid off." He finished his coffee. "I have to be going if I want to be back to work on time," he said and got up. "I will keep a close watch on everyone in that house. It shouldn't be that difficult. There's only Mrs. Hellman, Allan, Becky and maybe Grant left in the house. It seems I heard Grant say he was leaving this morning to go back to his place. He does not sound or act happy like the others. It is as if he expects something terrible to happen."

"He is correct, Paul. Something terrible is going to happen." Latimer walked him to the front door. Sue Ellen walked in before he could close it.

"Good morning y'all," she said with a bright smile. "I'm not late am I?"

"No, we were early. I even fixed coffee for you." Latimer went back into his office to pick up the bag with the glasses. "I'm on my way to the precinct. Do me a favor and tell Brighton I'm coming with some evidence for the Hellman case."

"I will do that, Latimer darlin'," Sue Ellen said as she filled her coffee cup.

Brighton was sitting in his office with his head in his hands when Latimer walked in. He looked dejected.

"I'm stumped with my case, Latimer. I hope you've come to help me." There was no smile on his face. "I don't think I can handle this job. As a matter of fact, I quite hate it. To live in fear of the Chief to produce results in record time and with limited resources, is not what I want to do for the rest of my life."

"What are you saying, Brighton?" Latimer asked.

"I'm going to quit the force. Hattie says it's ok with her. I can always get a security job somewhere that's not so stressful. She still has her job and together we can make enough to live on."

"You're serious, Kid?"

"Yes, I am. I was going to call you and tell you about it this week. I've been online every day looking for something."

"You do have ten years toward your pension. Are you sure you want to give that up?" Latimer asked.

"I'm sure. This is not for me." Brighton sounded dejected. "I think I'm a failure. It was so much easier when you were here. You always knew what to do."

"I think I still know what to do, Kid." Latimer leaned over and looked at him with a smile. "Come work for me. I'm making good money and I need someone I can trust and who works well with me. Come and be a private detective in my agency."

Brighton looked at Latimer in stunned silence. Finally, he managed to say," Are you serious?"

"I am totally serious, but only if I can call you Kid again. I can't stand it any other way." Latimer smiled.

"You can call me anything you want as long as I can work for you." His face was beaming with the brightest smile Latimer had ever seen on him.

"Of course I could call you Kevin. We'll see how it works out." Latimer stood up and they shook hands. "There is one more thing," he added after he sat back down, "I'm sixty-five and won't be able to work forever. I figure, by the time I finally retire, you'll have gained enough experience to do this on your own. If things work out the way I think they will, by that time you'll be a partner in the business anyway and can take over." Latimer leaned back with a satisfied smile. "This is turning out to be a good day all the way around if you find the fingerprints on here that I think will show us who the killer is." He handed Brighton the bag with the glasses. "Please have the precinct charge the Hellman estate for the cost."

"When can I get started at your office, Latimer?" Brighton asked. He sounded unsure of himself as if he still couldn't believe what just happened.

"How about giving the precinct enough notice so they can make arrangements to replace you. Never burn your bridges behind you when you leave a place. A month will do, I should think, unless they let you go earlier."

"That sounds great. I will talk to the Chief today and get the paperwork started." He sounded excited. "Just wait till I tell Hattie," he added as he walked out the door with the bag in his hand.

On the way home, Latimer felt like celebrating and stopped at the store to buy all the ingredients for a steak dinner. He was almost as excited as the Kid. It would be wonderful to have him at his side again. Latimer was thankful there was a spare room at the office. It wasn't much bigger than a broom closet, but Sue Ellen could buy some furniture at the thrift store and give Brighton his own office. It would do until he had earned his wings. Latimer had a feeling they would need a bigger building not too long in the future, at the rate things were going.

"I was hoping you had bought something for dinner," Glenda said when she got home from work an hour later. "I'm bushed. It was a hectic day. Cassie is taking on more responsibility and that means more work for me. I'm going to have to ask her for an assistant if it keeps up." She sank into her chair. "That isn't steak I smell, is it, honey?"

"It is. We're celebrating today. My business has just increased by fifty percent today," Latimer said. "I've hired Brighton as my assistant." He looked at her with a smile. "I beat you to it."

"What about his job at the force?" she asked.

"He doesn't like it and told me he was going to quit when I was at his office today. So I offered him a job and he took it. What am I saying? He nearly kissed my ring he was so excited." Latimer laughed. "We are both happy about it. With the other half of the fee I will soon be collecting from the Hellman estate, I can well afford him."

"Does that mean you have solved the case?" Glenda asked, surprised.

"I haven't solved it yet, but it shouldn't be but a few days."

"Who did it?"

"I'm not ready to say. Too many things have to happen first. I know they will, but I want to make sure." He brought the platter with two juicy steaks and put them on the table. "Come on, Mrs. Latimer, your dinner is served."

Two days went by and nothing happened. Latimer was beginning to get impatient. The fingerprint lab had not had time to check on his prints. A big case at the precinct demanded all their attention. Apparently his influence at the precinct wasn't what it once was, but in all probability, Inspector Brown made sure his case took precedent over Latimer's. Paul had not called either. He hated the waiting. Sue Ellen had already told him he was 'as crotchety as an old hound dog' and tried to ignore him.

His cell phone rang. It was Becky Hellman.

"Latimer, is there any way you could come to the house? I'm afraid something is wrong with Mom. She wants to see you." Becky sounded anxious.

"Of course, I'll be there in thirty minutes," he said. The time had come. He was sure of it.

"Please, come in, Sir," Paul said as he let Latimer in. "I think this is the day."

"You are right, it is, Paul. I've been waiting for this moment." Latimer followed Paul to the family room.

Becky was sitting in her mother's chair, staring out the window. Her face was drawn and sad as she said, "Mom is not doing well. It's more than just her usual illness. She looks terrible and won't get out of bed. I've had the doctor here and he can't find anything wrong with her other than her normal weakened condition. I know different. Something is terribly wrong. She hasn't been the same since Allan was let go."

"Where is Allan?" Latimer asked.

"He went to town to talk to someone about his new project. He's all excited about it." She looked at Latimer. "She wants you to talk to her."

"Becky, has your mom said anything?"

"No, but I have the feeling she's ready to tell you what it is we've all wanted to know. I've asked her many times, but she finally told me, when the time is right, she'll tell us all what it is." Becky got up and together they went upstairs to Mrs. Hellman's bedroom.

"It was dark in the room. Becky turned the light on. Patricia Hellman lay with her eyes closed, a small, thin shadow of her former self. She opened her eyes when they walked in and looked at Latimer.

"You've come to solve the case, haven't you, Mr. Latimer?" she said in a whisper. "It is time."

"Yes, it is, Mrs. Hellman. I think it would be best if all your children are present when you tell me the truth, don't you think?" he asked in a gentle tone.

"I don't think I can do that. I would prefer to have you and Paul with me when I tell you. There is a camera in the closet." She looked at Becky. "Why don't you check dear, and see if you can set it up to record what I have to say."

Becky opened the closet door. Latimer turned and called Paul to come up and join them. He asked him to help Becky set up the equipment. It took a few minutes until they had erected the small camera on a tri-pod and positioned it toward Patricia. Latimer checked it if it was working. It was.

"Becky, sweetheart, I want you to leave now, please. It is better that way." She reached over and stroked Becky's hair. "I love you."

Becky tried very hard to hide her tears as she walked out. She stopped just outside the door and left it ajar enough to be able to hear what was being said. Latimer saw what she was doing and nodded his approval.

"We are ready, Patricia. I'm going to turn the camera on now," he said as he walked over and pushed the button. The red light came on. "Patricia, you can talk now."

She raised herself up, looked directly into the camera and began in a low, weak voice.

"Just like your father, I would like to leave a video for all of you before I die. I want you to know how much I love you. My entire life has been spent caring for you and seeing to your needs. I have made many mistakes and I want to ask you to forgive me. The biggest one I ever made was to oppose my husband on how to raise our children. I thought love meant giving you everything you wanted. He understood, real love means giving you everything you needed. In the end, our disagreement in this area not only destroyed our marriage, but our lives as well. He told me he was going to divorce me, since I would not stop giving money to all of you behind his back. He saw his children being destroyed by my deception and the endless supply of money I gave to you. Every one of you turned into selfish, self centered and spoiled individuals who despised him, because he wouldn't give in to your endless materialism.

When I realized I would lose him and his money, I devised a plan to stop him. I arranged for a trip to the Amazon River. I had read in an article that they had poisons down there that hadn't even been discovered yet. I stole a prescription form from William's office and typed the request of bringing some medicine for research back with him and gave it to Allan. Eager to please his oldest brother, he did what it asked and purchased the medicine from a native down there. He had no idea I was the one who wrote it. William had nothing to do with it." Patricia's voice was getting weaker as she continued.

"When we returned from the Amazon, Allan stored the bottles in his medicine cabinet so he could give them to William. I took them before he could talk to his brother. I had to tell him the truth and what I wanted to use it for or he would have talked to William. At first he was upset, but finally, he agreed to go along with my plan. After several months, I started putting tiny amounts of the poison in William's food, every other day at first and then every day. Slowly, he became more and more ill. It was so gradual, no one noticed, until it was too late. The final dose finally made his heart fail. By the time William realized something was wrong, he was too weak to do anything about it. That's when he called Gary Norton and had the video made. He had no idea it was me who poisoned him.

You will ask, why did I do it? I did it for you, my children. I had to plan ahead for the day William would divorce me and then I couldn't give you what you so desperately wanted, money. I knew you would love him more than me, because without him, I wouldn't be the one you relied on.

The reason I involved Allan was very simple. With the money William left me, I could afford the best lawyers and they would get him off if he didn't say anything. I knew he wouldn't turn his own mother in. Once he was pronounced innocent by a jury, he couldn't ever be tried again. No one would continue to look for another suspect, but blame the jury for letting him go. Even if he had been convicted, I would have come forward and told what I did and that he was innocent. Either way, he would go free. As for me, I would have killed myself before I would go to prison." She stopped for a moment as if in pain and then continued.

"The reason I killed Henry was he found my notebook where I outlined my plan. He also found one of the bottles of the poison and took it from me. When he told me he would have to go to the police if I didn't turn myself in, I had no choice but to kill him that day with a large dose. After he went to the hospital, I looked everywhere for the notebook, but never found it.

I kept the second bottle of the poison for this day. When I heard you come in Mr. Latimer, I took the rest of it and soon I will be dead. I don't know if God will ever forgive me. Now I know I have done a terrible wrong, but then I thought I was fighting for my children's way of life.

After I tried to take my life the last time, I shared with Grant what I had done. He made me promise not to tell anyone, because he didn't want Allan or me to go to prison. That is no longer possible. My life is over and I will have to take my punishment for all eternity." She began to cry as the pain was beginning to overwhelm her body.

"You can still be forgiven, Patricia," Latimer said. "God will forgive you if you ask Him to right now." He leaned over her and took her hand. "Will you ask Him and then give Him your life?"

"There is no way He could ever love a person like me, Mr. Latimer. It is too late for me."

"No, it isn't. There is still time. Please, Patricia, just ask Him." He looked at her as she started to convulse. "Paul, call 911, hurry!" he yelled.

It was too late. Patricia died two hours later in the hospital without ever regaining consciousness. Latimer was there in the room, together with the children. No one spoke. Allan held her hand and cried uncontrollably. He looked broken. The others did not speak to him, but looked on with a mixture of anger, sorrow and shock. Latimer could tell they blamed him for her death and the death of their father and Henry. He could have stopped all of this tragedy, but decided to stay silent in order to inherit the money.

When Patricia stopped breathing, William checked her pulse, and without another word walked out of the room. The others followed slowly, one after another, until only Allan and Latimer were left in the room.

"I am guilty, Latimer. I could've stopped her and didn't. I will never live that down for the rest of my life. The only thing I can do is to make up for what I've done and use the money for good. It will be my life's work, not because God won't forgive me, He has. I want to help others less fortunate like my dad wanted me to. I will make it his legacy."

Two weeks later, Gary Norton called the children into his office for the reading of Patricia's Will. He had also invited Latimer to attend the meeting. It was a sad group of people who sat around the large, oblong table, waiting for the lawyer to come in. No one said a word. Allan sat alone.

"Good morning, Ladies and Gentlemen," Gary Norton said as he walked in with a folder in hand. "Please accept my condolences on your mother's death. What a tragic thing to happen. The reason this has taken so long, your mother's Will had to be considered before I could figure out the amount of money each of you will receive. She leaves the house and the grounds of the estate to you, William, as the oldest. It is her wish that you raise your children there. All other properties left from her holdings are to be sold and the proceeds divided among the rest of you. The fifty million from her recent inheritance from your father is to be divided among you children. That brings your inheritance to ten million dollars for each of you from your mother's Will. It will take some time for the legal matters to be taken care of. You will receive the money from your father's Will today in the amount of forty million each since it had to be divided by five instead of four." He handed each of them an envelope. They took it without saying a word and left in silence.

Gary Norton looked at Latimer, who was the only one left.

"William was right when he hired you. You have earned your fee. Here it is." He handed Latimer an envelope. "I hope I can refer you to any of my clients who need a private detective at times. I am impressed with your skill, integrity and honesty, Mr. Latimer. Those are rare qualities in today's world." He shook his hand and escorted him to the front door. "If I can ever be of service Sir, do not hesitate to call me," he added and shook Latimer's hand.

The next day Latimer got the report from the fingerprint lab. Patricia Hellman's prints were on the bottle. He put down the report with a sigh. She had given not only her life, but her soul for her children.

His cell phone rang. Allan was on the line.

"Could I come by Latimer?"

"Of course you can, Allan. I will be waiting."

Latimer walked around the desk and hugged Allan. He pointed to the chair in front of his desk.

"Have a seat, what can I do for you?"

"I have come to ask you a favor, Mr. Latimer. As you can imagine, I don't have very many friends left in this world after what I've done. I had to change my phone number because of several threatening calls. Tomorrow I move into a new place, because my brother has told me to leave immediately. He won't even talk to me. My other siblings have not been in touch at all. I am alone." He shifted in his seat. "That is not what I came here for." He looked at Latimer with a mixture of sadness and hope. "I am creating a thirty million dollar trust fund for the creation of a non-profit organization here in Glenridge. My goal is to build a village with several shelters and rehab facilities for those in desperate need. It will be called "HIS PERFECT LEGACY" and will be dedicated to the memory of William Carl Hellman."

"That sounds wonderful, Allan. Your father would be so proud of you," Latimer said. "I cannot think of anything else that would undo in some measure what you have done."

"The reason I'm here, Mr. Latimer, I would like for you to be on the Board of Directors of this foundation and help in the area of those who have been in jail or prison." He looked at Latimer with a question on his face. "Would you consider doing it?"

"I absolutely will. Not only that, there is someone who I will speak to that will be a part of this in the area of drug rehabilitation."

"Who?" Allan sounded eager.

"Your sister Becky."

"She won't even talk to me, Mr. Latimer, least of all help me." Allan sounded sure.

"Give me a few days and I will get in touch with her. I know she'll do it." Latimer smiled. "Who else are you going to ask to be on the Board?"

"Gary Norton. He has agreed already. He will be our legal counsel."

"How about Cassie Anscott, she's a good friend of mine. With her stature and the financial power of Anscott Laboratories behind her, she would be a great asset to the foundation. To have her as a board member would give the foundation a legitimacy you can't get anywhere else. Do you want me to ask her?" Latimer looked at Allan with smile. "You see, you're not alone, Allan. There are many people who will help and support you once they see what you're trying to do, even your family."

Latimer was on his way to see Becky at her condo late the following afternoon. She let him in with a big smile.

"How good it is to see you, Latimer. I've been meaning to call you and thank you for all you've done for me and my family. If I can ever do anything to make it up to you, let me know." She sounded good.

"I'm glad you said that. There is something you can do, maybe not for me, but for your brother Allan."

"You are kidding, right? I never want to see him again. He is despicable and I'm sorry I have to admit to anyone he's related to me. I'll do anything but that." Her voice sounded almost like the old Becky, harsh and cynical.

"Before you make up your mind, let me remind you that you were in a situation equally as hopeless and despicable to your siblings, remember?" He looked at her with a faint smile. "You changed and they took you back. Can you do the same for Allan?" he added.

"I didn't kill anyone."

"Just yourself, what's the difference?"

She looked at him, stunned.

"I never thought of it that way. What is it you want me to do for Allan?"

"He has created a thirty million dollar trust fund to create a non-profit organization to build a charitable village with different outreach clinics and shelters called HIS PERFECT LEGACY in memory of your father. At the moment he is trying to find people to be on the executive board of this organization. I suggested, you might be the perfect candidate in the area of a drug rehab clinic." Latimer leaned back in his chair and waited.

Becky looked at him with a strange look. After a long time she said, "He really means it, doesn't he? He is going to try to make up for what he did?"

"Yes, he is, Becky," Latimer said. "Jail time combined with the video, have changed him from a spoiled, obnoxious brat into a responsible human being. He is proving it with this project. Will you help him?"

"You are absolutely sure he means it?" Becky sounded doubtful.

"Do you mean what you said about your life?" Latimer asked.

She sat quietly for a long time.

"You do have a way with words, Latimer." She leaned forward. "I'll tell you what, I will talk to him and see for myself if I can work with a man who agreed with my mother to kill two people just to get a lot of money."

"He is ready to come and see you to discuss it, Becky. All you have to do is call him." Latimer reached for his cell phone. "By the way, he has a new number because of threatening phone calls. I will give it to you." He took a piece of paper and wrote it down and handed it to her.

"The rest is up to you. Remember, forgiveness is worthless without actions."

She took the number and put it on the coffee table.

"I will think about this and then decide."

When Latimer left, he had no idea if she would do it.

Chapter 28

Three days later, Latimer got a phone call from Allan. There would be a meeting on Saturday for the people who had agreed to participate in the project at a downtown restaurant called the "The Old Inn". Latimer arrived promptly at noon. He was shown into a small meeting room. To his astonishment he found Grant, Sylvia and Becky there. Gary Norton and Cassie Anscott Sanders smiled at him when he walked in. Allan stood at the head of the table talking with Peter Bellami. Pastor Nathaniel of New Life Church walked in after him.

Allan stepped up to the podium and tapped on the mike.

"Everyone, please, take a seat."

He waited for everyone to sit down before he went on.

"My name is Allan Hellman. I would like to start out by stating unequivocally that I am the least of you in this room trying to help the least in our community. All through the Bible God has used thieves and murderers to get his work done. We know them as King David, the thief on the cross, and the Apostle Peter who denied Christ three times, just to name a few. That puts me in good company." He cleared his throat before he went on.

"I want to thank you for coming. To tell you the truth, I wouldn't have been surprised if none of you had showed up. Pastor Nathaniel, would you come up and say a prayer for this meeting, this project and for those who are here to help make it possible?" He stepped aside and let the pastor pray. After he was done, Allan took the microphone again.

"What I want to do is explain what I have in mind, and then allow all of you to share ideas and resources how you could add to it. Before I do that, let me make something very clear. I realize you did not agree to help with this project because of me, but you're doing this in spite of me. I have done a terrible thing and I take full responsibility for it. That said, this project is to fulfill my father's wish for my life. In a video of his last Will he urged me to do volunteer work to find out how the other side lives. I did better than that, I became part of the other side. Instead of becoming bitter and angry, I suddenly realized I had no excuse for what I did, other than greed and being spoiled by unlimited riches. My father's video, the hardships of my time in jail and my mother's death made me understand that the only way I could become the person my father knew I could be, was to do what he asked me to do. I want to work and provide for those who have less than I do and give them an environment where they can be given a chance at a decent life. This is as much my chance as it is theirs. I thank all of you for wanting to be a part of His Perfect Legacy. Together we can make a difference in the lives of those who are less fortunate than we are."

No one had noticed Dr. Hellman standing by the door. He waited until Allan was finished and then walked forward and took the microphone.

"My name is Dr. William Hellman. I heard about this meeting from Gary Norton." He looked at Allan. "I never imagined, little brother, you could actually change and become someone Dad would've been proud of." He smiled. "I have come to make a suggestion to those of you in the family who want to be a part of this project. In the estate our parents have left all of us, there is a tract of fifty-five acres originally destined for a new housing development on the edge of Glenridge. Since Mother's Will says we have to sell it, I'm here to suggest we donate it to Allan's project to be used for his new village. The Lord knows all of us need a tax break." He turned to his siblings with a questioning look. "What do you say? Raise your hands if this meets with your approval."

Four hands went up.

"That settles it then. Gary, why don't you draw up the papers and we'll all sign it." He actually looked a little embarrassed as he stepped away from the mike and walked toward the door.

"Wait, William," Allan said as he jumped up and rushed toward his brother. "Thank you." They hugged. "Stay and be part of the Executive Board. We could use medical advice when we start the clinic for the indigents."

William looked at Allan for a moment and slowly turned to sit down with the rest of them at the table.

Latimer watched in amazement as the people in the room were catching the vision of what was in Allan Hellman's heart.

The End

If you have enjoyed this book, would you please take the time to go on Amazon.com and write a review. I would so appreciate it. Your comments make the difference between success and failure for any author.

I have also written a WWII historical novel about the experiences of my mother as she flees from the East to escape the Russian front right into the carpet bombing of the Allies during the last six months of the war in Nazi Germany. "**When the East Wind Blows**" has a 4.5 star rating and is available for Kindle.

To buy it in paperback please go to my website: **www.BarbaraHMartin.com**, where you can see other books I have written or engage me as a speaker for your organization, conference or club. I have been a professional speaker for over twenty years and have traveled widely with my books.